SETH COOK REES
THE WARRIOR-SAINT

By

PAUL S. REES

"No pain, no palm; no thorns, no throne; no gall, no glory; no cross, no crown."

—WILLIAM PENN

ISBN 0-88019-213-5

Schmul Publishing Co., Inc.
Wesleyan Book Club
1987
Salem, Ohio

Printed by
Old Paths Tract Society Inc.
Shoals, Indiana 47581

TO

MRS. SETH C. REES

BY

HER SON

SETH COOK REES

PREFACE

SETH REES kept no journal. For only six or seven years of his life did he make regular entries in a diary. He was more interested in contributing to the making of history than he was in recording it. He did, however, leave some reminiscences that have greatly aided in filling in the outline of his life. These have been supplemented by personal references and incidents that appeared from time to time in such of his writings as sermons, articles and reports.

Part I, which tells the running story of his earthly tenure has been made as autobiographical as possible. Seth Rees has been made to speak for Seth Rees. Part II, designated as "Analytical," undertakes to supply an element of appraisal that is far more detached and less subjective than anything which, in the nature of the case, the author could hope to achieve. In Part III it is again the voice of "THE WARRIOR-SAINT." Two sermons have been selected which, it is hoped, will make it true of him, as it has been of so many of God's valiants who have gone before him, that he "being dead yet speaketh."

The author is deeply grateful for the cooperation of Rev. John Pennington, Rev. G. A. Hodgin and Rev. Paul W. Thomas, contributors of Part II. Since the completion of the manuscript the first member of this assisting trio has passed into the presence of his Lord. He was by ten years the senior of the man in whose memory he has written herein. Their friendship, well begun in this land, now blooms immortal in that fair Yonderland where it is always morning.

Thanks are due, also, to the many friends of Seth Rees who have provided me with valuable information—confirming or correcting points in question, settling dates, recalling incidents, commenting on traits of character, and so on. Imperfections and inaccuracies that have survived the earnest endeavor to avoid them must have the reader's generous charity.

It should be added that the appreciations found in the chapter entitled "IN MEMORIAM" are selected from many that appeared in the press and were received by mail. No one was asked to write for this chapter. Had they been requested to do so, many of Seth Rees's warmest friends and admirers, whose names do not appear, would have been delighted, I am sure, to add their tribute.

To the son, whose father's God-crowned figure moves and, let us hope, in some measure breathes through the following pages, this book has been in a dual sense a labor of love: wistful love for the father who has gone, worshipful love for the Christ who remains.

P. S. R.

KANSAS CITY, MISSOURI
CHRISTMAS DAY
1933

CONTENTS

PART I

BIOGRAPHICAL

CONTENTS

CONTENTS

PART II

ANALYTICAL

PART III

INSPIRATIONAL

TWO SERMONS

By REV. SETH C. REES

ILLUSTRATIONS

Part I
BIOGRAPHICAL

SETH COOK REES THE WARRIOR-SAINT

CHAPTER I

ENLISTMENT

"You came into the world crying while all around you were smiling; so live that you may go out of the world smiling while all around you are weeping."

These words, part of an Eastern prayer inscribed on the walls of an ancient temple, found certain fulfilment in the life of Seth Cook Rees. Born at Westfield, Indiana, twenty miles north of Indianapolis, August 6, 1854, he was the first child of his mother, Luzena Rees, and the tenth child of his father, Zechariah Rees. But if all the children of a former marriage, together with the happy parents and the congratulating neighbors, were smiling at the coming of this baby boy, their number was extremely small compared with the hosts who, at the end of his pilgrimage, sorrowed at his departure. Seventy-eight years after that August natal day at Westfield, the news of his death, at Pasadena, California, began a world-circling journey, was received with regret by countless thousands who had come under the influence of his ministry and was announced in the religious press by such captions as that of Dr. John Paul in *The Christian Witness:* "A World Figure Moves Heavenward." This memoir is a partial record of the years that lie between—a combination of romance and epic centering in that divine goodness and strength expressed in the Pauline confession, "By the grace of God I am what I am."

Three-quarters of a century ago the towns of Westfield and Salem, in Indiana, were perhaps the largest Quaker settlements in the world. To the latter the two Rees brothers, father and uncle of Seth Rees, had made their way from North Carolina in the van of the westward march of the pioneers. They carried in their veins the singing blood of old Wales.

The ancient Welsh spelling of the name was Rhys. In the 11th century Rhys Ap Tewdor was Prince of North Wales. Rhys Ap Tewdor Mawr was King of South Wales. The Rhys coat-of-arms was sculptured on the west front of Llanwenog Church in Cardiganshire and on the tombs of the dead. In 1599 descendants of the South House of Rhys emigrated to England, where the spelling was changed to Rees. In 1700 the Rev. Charles Rees and several brothers, sons of the Rev. David Ap Rees, pastor of the Presbyterian Church at Southwark, London, landed at Newcastle, Delaware. One of the brothers settled in Pennsylvania, from where his son, David, emigrated to Mecklenberg County, North Carolina. To his union with Mary Polk, whose father, Robert Polk, was an ancestor of President James K. Polk, ten children were born. From this group of Reeses came Zechariah, father of Seth Rees.

It is well known that about the close of the first quarter of the 19th century there was a large exodus of Quakers from North Carolina. Slavery was odious to them. They would neither traffic in it nor look with tolerance upon it. Hence their departure from the banks of the Yadkin River for the free soil of the western states, notably Ohio, Indiana and Iowa. Presumably this was the main motive prompting the westward trek of Zechariah Rees and his brother. At all events they were among the frontiersmen who found the commonwealth of Indiana very much as the Indians had left it. Having pushed their way to the little settlement of Salem, they were the first to cut a wagon road north from that point into the virgin forests of the "Hoosier State."

Near the south edge of the Westfield of today is a cemetery. Here was the original Rees farm. Here upon the knoll, with a fine spring of water near by, Zechariah Rees built the first home in the district. If it was not splendid, it was at least spacious, as houses went in those days. It was made of logs, consisted mainly of two large rooms and stood, with its long porch fronting the sun-rise, amid a leafy setting of white oaks, poplars, maples and wild cherries. This was the simple but wholesome center of the life and toil of Zechariah Rees and his dainty southern wife to whom he was fervently devoted.

Right nobly did they strive to serve their God, their family, their church and their community. A father who was a generous provider, who cured his meat with great care and each fall hung up thirty-two shoulders and thirty-two hams as a part of the winter's supply; who possessed an enlightened social conscience that led him to promote the freedom and uplift of the black folk and to serve as a generous patron of education in his own township; who "loved righteousness and hated iniquity"; such a father it was whom affectionate children delighted to recall long years afterward. A mother who, when widowed by the death of her first husband, had learned to ply the needle with skill, and who did much with her own hands to clothe her family; whose gracious hospitality made her home a sort of headquarters for visiting Quaker ministers; whose culinary contributions towards the entertainment of a Quarterly Meeting would extend at least as far as twenty-seven pies baked on a single Saturday; who, although she did no audible praying, lived a life of quiet, impressive spiritual devotion; such a mother it was who enshrined herself deathlessly in the memory of her sons and daughters.

"The first event (says Seth Rees in some autobiographical notes) which fastened itself so lastingly upon my mind that it has never been forgotten, occurred when I was only twenty-five months old. It was a visit to the State Fair seventeen miles from our humble country home. To me the most fascinating thing of all that may have been in those ample fair grounds was watching the trotting horses as they swept the circle, passing so closely to where my dear old Quaker father had located me. Young as I was, I became a great admirer of 'Sweepstakes' and of the red ribbon she wore. From that hour to this I have been ready to take off my hat to any thing or person that passes under the line with credit in any pursuit as innocent as those competitions were seventy-five years ago. To many a railroad locomotive have I lifted my hat and bowed in appreciation of her ability to climb the mountains, span the rivers, sweep the plains and drop me at my destination three minutes ahead of her scheduled time; and more than once has she answered my congratulations by blowing off steam enough to assure me she could do it again. From the time of the races of 1856 to this hour my whole being has revolted against defeat. Failure must not be. Win or die! And more than once to die has been my greatest victory.

"The 'big room' where I first saw the light—first kicked, cooed, crowed and smiled—was the size of my first world. For long, bleak winter months the four walls of that room bounded all the world that I knew. Later the lines were moved out to the yard and garden fence. What a world! What liberty! What childish glee! Then my bounds were enlarged to include the 'sugar orchard'—for that was what we called it—where father tapped six hundred great maple trees each springtime. We drew sap enough to make maple sugar and molasses for the whole community. What a time we had boiling the sap day and night, making a pulling wax and all the rest. It was fun alive—innocent fun to give away.

"The 'big room,' twenty feet square, was furnished with the quaintest old things you ever saw. The great double beds were so high that a ladder was used to scale the bed rail and tumble into a feather bed and sink out of sight. The beds must needs be high, for under each of them was a double trundle bed that was pulled out at bed time and occupied by juniors. There were two large old rockers made by hand by John Boone, presumably of the Daniel Boone family. There was no 'wear out' to the furniture of those days. There was the famous old hand-made cradle that rocked all the little Reeses to sleep a thousand times. Under the tall, long wooden mantle was a big mud-and-brick-lined open fireplace with its swinging iron cranes and hooks from which were suspended the pots in which the water was heated to bathe the little regiment of Reeses.

"For many years the principal evening light flickered from this open fireplace. By that light mother cut and made, patched and darned, our homespun wearing apparel, while we children studied our lessons, roasted apples, cracked nuts or popped corn. One of us was well occupied feeding the blaze with scaley hickory bark. Our only other light was furnished by home-made candles and tallow dips. One day father came home from town with a glass coal-oil lamp. (The word 'kerosene' had not been coined so far as we knew.) There was some excitement that day. We could hardly wait for the winter darkness to settle upon us. When the coveted hour came and the beautiful lamp was lighted, we each had a book or paper with which to test the power of the light by determining how far back in the room we could see to read. That memorable night will live forever. Electricity was unknown to us, except as it flashed from the ragged thunder cloud or sparkled under friction.

"What did we have to eat? Well, we had plenty of potatoes baked in hot ashes, and apples roasted in front of the fire. We had lots of apples. We had two big farms a mile apart. Once, however, we had such drought that nothing could grow and we had no money with which to buy white flour. What bread we had was made of 'shorts.' That is what it was called. I suppose it was the best thing for us. When they ground the wheat in those days, they first took off the bran, which nobody wanted except for the hogs. They returned it to us as a gift. After the bran was removed they ground the white flour, which sold at a price so high we could not afford to eat it. Only the rich could buy it. Then from the heart of the wheat came the 'shorts.' So wheat taken to the mill was carried away in three parts: white flour, shorts and bran.

"I was brought up to arise at four a. m., winter and summer. In winter four o'clock was a good while before daylight, especially if it was twenty degrees below zero. No difference about that, I had to get up. We often awoke with snow over the bed. We had log fires for heat. It seemed to me I had to chop wood nearly all day to get enough to burn at night. But there were other things to do. I had six or eight horses to feed, curry and bed, besides caring for perhaps twenty head of cattle, forty head of sheep and forty or fifty head of hogs. All this had to be done with a lantern before daylight.

"Daytime work varied, especially in the winter. Sometimes it would be to cut a tree, four feet at the butt, into ten-foot lengths and split it into rails for our fences. One time I cut down a white oak that was 300 years old. I counted the growth. I cut it into the right length and used a crowbar to 'rove' it into staves. I then took the staves—I could haul about a thousand of them with two horses—to Indianapolis, twenty miles away. I made staves to get money to get married. They called them oil-barrel staves but that was just a camouflage; they made whisky barrels out of them. I would get up at one a. m., leave home at two and reach Indianapolis about eight. Then I would hunt the best stave market. They would give me about $20.00 per thousand. By the time I got all unloaded it would be about two p. m. and I would get home about dark—or later if I had to do some shopping for my new bride."

Reminiscing briefly concerning his parents, Seth Rees said:

"Father was brought up in a distillery. When a lad there were rush seasons when he would not have his clothes off for six weeks at a time. Nearly all the farmers had their own stills, grew their own fruit for peach and apple brandy and their own grain for rye and corn whisky. The curse of God seemed to be on grandfather's old distillery. He could not keep out of debt. When in trouble he would go to father for help, and father always responded until one eventful day when there came a sudden change in his life. Though he could neither read nor write at that time, and had no one to read the Bible to him, the blessed Holy Ghost, without human instrumentality, led him to Christ in wonderful conversion. The next time grandfather came to him for financial aid father said, 'Only on one condition—that the old still shall never be fired again.' Those infernal flames went out forever.

"One of the sweetest memories of my childhood was when father or mother would take from the shelf the great old family Bible and read its great stories of creation, of Christ, of Joseph, David, Daniel, Paul and so on. Then we would all go into a solemn Quaker silence for several minutes. No audible prayer was offered. To them it was family worship; to us it was a good example. Though I never heard either of my parents pray until after I was converted, I know that they did and that their prayers moved heaven. When a wayward young man, no difference how late I returned home, I found mother sitting in the big arm chair. She never disrobed until her boy was in bed. Will you question that she prayed or that her prayers were heard? But for those nights of prayer, I might have been in hell fifty years ago. Oh, Mother, Mother! What a dear sweet word!"

The Society of Friends maintained an academy at Westfield. It was this institution that furnished Seth Rees with all the schooling he received beyond the learning of the three R's.

At nineteen occurred the miracle of the New Birth. We shall report it in the language of its subject's personal testimony:

"I regret to record that early in my 'teens I threw off the lines of restraint, and for several years a wild, impetuous, evil spirit carried me into sin. It was under the faithful, fiery ministry of the sainted Calvin W. Pritchard, in the third month, 1873, that I was put under deep and pungent conviction, and gloriously converted to God.

"The 'anxious seat,' or 'penitent form,' was not then used in our meetings, but at the close of a sermon preached 'with the Holy Ghost sent down from heaven,' all were requested to stand who desired the prayers of God's people. To the utter astonishment of a large congregation, almost all of whom knew me personally, I arose. I had not at that time the most remote idea of being converted. In fact, I had no thought that it was possible for me to be saved. I remember distinctly of saying to myself, 'I will give them a good subject to try their hand on.' No further request was made, and no one spoke to me about the step I had taken.

"To a similar invitation the next evening I stood up, more because I had done so the night before than anything else. But now I began 'to feel serious,' and when on First-day night a different call was made and all were asked to arise who sincerely desired to become Christians, in company with a number of others I promptly responded. Nothing more was said to me, either publicly or privately, but the dear Holy Spirit suggested to me that I attend the day meeting on Second-day morning.

"As I entered the meeting-house yard a neighbor said: 'Will thee come and sit with me?' and without waiting for an answer he led the way to a seat much farther forward than I had been accustomed to occupy since I was a boy. I had not long been seated when the Spirit fell upon the congregation, and the meeting proved to be one of testimony and confession. When the meeting was well under way, a strange power came over me and I arose and confessed that I was an awful sinner. I was not on my feet thirty seconds, but I sat down a saint! Up to that time I had not attempted to pray. I had not shed a tear. Now my eyes were fountains; I wept like rain. The complexion of everything changed. Every blade of grass, every drop of water and every bird of forest and field, seemed to dance with delight."

CHAPTER II

THE WHOLE ARMOR

SETH REES was converted in March (1873). The following August he made his first attempt at preaching.

"The last week of August (he says) was the Quaker Quarterly Meeting (Westfield, Ind.). It was said that there were 8000 people there by count. It was a place of preachers. There were perhaps 1500 in the church. The Friends Academy, on the same grounds, was filled. There were 3000 in the grove. Back and forth the crowds moved. I got about half way between the church and a new well that had just been dug. The dirt had been thrown up in a pile almost as high as a man's shoulders. It being the last week in August, and hot, they had employed a big coal-black negro to pump water for the crowds. There he stood all day, with a dozen bright, new tin cups, supplying water for the tired, thirsty people.

"There must have been 200 or 300 folks waiting for their turn to get a drink, and hundreds more within hearing. The Spirit spoke to this lad and said, 'You get up on that pile of dirt and preach to this people.' I had never preached. I had witnessed just a little. We were always told to be very careful not to get ahead of the Spirit. I walked down to the church, desiring to obey God. Then I walked back up by the pump, where I knew I should preach. I went the second time down by the church, and prayed. I was trying the spirits. I do not know how many times I passed that pump, always impressed with the same feeling: 'I must get on that dirt and preach.'

"Finally I felt clear and, pressing my way past people, I climbed on the pile of dirt, and began. I can't tell what I said. I do not recall that I had a text. It was my first attempt to preach. When I was through and got down off the dirt-pile, another preacher climbed into a spring wagon and continued the service. Almost before I had considered what my calling was, the Meeting of which I was a member had acknowledged my gift and 'recorded' me a minister of the Gospel of Christ.

"I conferred not with flesh and blood, but under the immediate and perceptible guidance of the Spirit I went into schoolhouses and churches, preaching wherever I could—Pleasant View, Grassy Branch, East Branch, Poplar Ridge, Eagletown, Black Creek, Walnut Ridge, Thorntown, Wabash, Marion and other places. At first I worked all week and preached on Sundays. In the leaves of the forest I would cry and pray, and pray and cry, and make my preparation. At some places they seemed glad to have me; at others I knew I wasn't wanted. I often had opposition from the conservatives, but the liberals invited me. Entertainment was always good. The Quakers always seemed to have enough to eat.

"At one place the supervisor gave me permission to use the school building. I went from house to house and told them there was going to be a revival. The people came. I preached—or thought I did. I told them of Jesus, and they fell down, in church and out, and prayed and cried, and got up and shouted. That shout of 'sins forgiven' was new in that neighborhood. One big, tall fellow shouted and laughed and made a big fuss. In a few days he died, and died happy, and went to heaven.

"I heard of another needy place, nine miles away. But I had no money on which to go. I had a little carpet bag and a couple of shirts that mother had given me, two or three collars and a handkerchief or two. I said I could find the place; I would walk. I decided that the nearest way would be to follow the railroad, so I took to the ties. I got pretty tired but rested along the way. We had a revival. A great one!

"I was too noisy for many of the Quakers. I left home one midnight and took the train for a point two hundred miles distant. When I arrived in the old church yard, the Quaker pastor met me with the stern challenge: 'Art thou he that troubleth Israel?' I stayed for two weeks, however, and some of those Quaker folks were really converted."

It was in one of these early meetings that the "boy preacher" met Hulda Johnson, his companion in marriage and his partner in ministry across two dynamic decades. The suitor shall tell his own story:

"When I was a young man, it was quite common for the youths of my age to travel on horse-back. I chanced to have an unusually fine riding horse, on which, one day, I started for Cherry Grove, seventy-five miles distant, to visit my uncle and his family. When I arrived, it happened that a young lady of seventeen or eighteen, Hulda Johnson, was at their house. As I loped up to the gate and their attention was directed my way, she laughingly said (as I later learned), 'There comes the boy I'm going to marry some day.' We had never met. After being together awhile that day, our parting was with friendly feelings. There was no meeting again, no correspondence, for some time. She was a backslider and, at that time, I had not been converted. A few months later I gave my heart to God and soon was preaching.

"It was as a very young preacher that I came to Cherry Grove for a two weeks' meeting. Nevertheless, the power of the Lord was upon the services. There were seventy good cases of salvation. One of these was the reclamation of Hulda Johnson. She had felt a call to preach but, in her backslidden state, was living just as others were. Very soon after her spiritual restoration she began to preach. She was extremely timid but deeply determined. This was an evangelistic campaign for which I received twenty-five cents, and walked three miles to the train.

"I saw no more of Miss Johnson for months, but when I heard of her, she was preaching with increasing evidence of her gifts. The local Meeting in which she held her membership recorded her as a minister. Meanwhile I was evangelizing in Ohio. The months passed. And then, as we Quakers would say, I felt led to write her a very small letter. I didn't think it would receive an answer, although I sincerely hoped it would. It was promptly answered, and through correspondence we became very much attached. I think I visited her only once between the time of the Cherry Grove meeting and our engagement."

Thus unfolded the unique romance which, in December, 1876, led Seth Rees and Hulda Johnson to the marriage altar. The effect, however, was vastly more than that of uniting two lives in mutual affection and home-making. Extending over a period of twenty-two years, it was a beautiful and beneficent association in spiritual calling and ministry. If Hulda Rees was naturally inclined to the private life of a wife and mother, she was supernaturally impelled to the public life of a Christian minister. Like Catherine Booth, she was a balanced soul in whom domestic virtues and platform gifts developed apace. The latter as we have seen, were early recognized by those in authority in the church of which she was a member. She almost invariably accompanied her husband in his labors.

Of their first united adventures in evangelism it is recorded: "In 1877 there were meetings held at Greenwood, Hadley and Poplar Run, Indiana. God graciously poured out His Spirit and many were converted and reclaimed."

About three years after their marriage, when their first son, Byron Johnson, was a babe of eighteen months, they were invited by Hulda Rees's father to make his home theirs, and to take charge of his farm which was located at Cherry Grove, Indiana. In this there lay, as it later developed, something of a snare. Less than two years of farming brought on a crisis. The chief contributing factors were, first, uncongenial relations between father-in-law and son-in-law and, second, a distinct summons of the Inner Voice. Speaking of the closing weeks of this period, Seth Rees records:

"God was talking to me and I didn't know it. I would work all day between plow-handles, and weep, and didn't know why. Then God told me that He hadn't called me to farm but to preach. (I had preached every chance I got, all over the country on Sundays.) Father Johnson was giving me one-half of all I made on the farm. Of course I had to give him notice. I told him that I was called to preach and that I would never farm again."

From Cherry Grove to Walnut Ridge, Indiana, is not a long journey—less than seventy-five miles. Such was the move that in 1880 brought Seth and Hulda Rees and their two boys—a second son, Loring Walter, was born while they were residing at Cherry Grove—to their first pastorate.

"I had held a series of meetings there (runs another reminiscence) and the leading Friends asked, 'Wouldn't thee come here and be our pastor?' I said I might if the Lord led me to do so. In the spring we decided to go. There was very little in the way of house furnishings to ship. We had a high chair for the baby and a few things that had been given to us. Much of what we had been using belonged to our relatives. Into a wagon we loaded what little we possessed, and went to the station to ship it. When we unloaded on the station platform, somehow the high chair was placed too near the tracks. A train came along and smashed it. It was the best piece of furniture we had. I didn't have sense enough to put in a claim for it.

"The proceeds from my half of the crop had given us a little money. A mile from the church there was a four-room house, into which we moved at a rental of $5.00 per month.

The furniture was scarce; we had not a yard of carpet. After a few days a Quaker lady brought my wife a sewing rocker. She was considered a fanatic by some, but not by us; we thought she had good religion. She helped us out.

"It wasn't long until my money gave out. My wife had agreed with me that I should not rely on secular work. Part of my money went for books. We were down to nearly nothing. One morning we got around the breakfast table with only enough to eat for the children. There wasn't a cent in the house. There was one thing we could do, and did. We had family prayer. On our knees we wept for joy. We felt we were in this place for Jesus. Mrs. Rees was a good singer; she sang more than usual that morning. Then she washed what few dishes had been used. As I dried them she sang the sweetest that I ever heard her sing. She put the dishes away. There wasn't food enough left to feed a cat. But we were happy; we were trusting. By eight o'clock the house-work was all done."

Unfortunately the story, as left in Seth Rees's written recollections, breaks off at this point. His relatives and friends, however, have heard him tell how wonderfully God carried the little family over the crisis. A load of provisions came before night-fall! Trials there were, but triumphs too, as their first pastorate, with its rugged initiation, built sturdy stuff into the souls of this preacher-pair.

Ten years have now gone busily by since that night in the Westfield Meeting House when, in rising to confess his sins, Seth Rees got his "head out of time into eternity" and was "born from above." His gifts as a preacher have, meanwhile, brought him constantly wider recognition. His evangelistic ministry has been abundant in evidences of anointing from God and effectiveness with men. Doors of larger opportunity are opening to him.

Notwithstanding all this, the young preacher is seriously disturbed, particularly on occasions, by certain features of his own spiritual life. A crisis is impending. As Israel came to Kadesh-barnea, Jacob to Peniel, Isaiah to the temple vision and the disciples to Pentecost, so Seth Rees was brought to face the necessity, within himself, and the offer, from his Divine Lord, of what he was subsequently to proclaim with flaming fervor to countless thousands of believers—the mighty Baptism with the Holy Ghost and Fire. Let the story be told in his own words:

"I found the motions of evil within me. I was not a little surprised to discover that there was a sin-principle remaining in my breast, which mocked, persecuted and threatened the new life. It required great devotion and much prayer and watching to remain in victory. I had seasons of great depression of spirit, and sometimes suffered temporary defeat. At other times I would ascend to mounts of rapture and ecstasy. I know now that I was led to profess sanctification when I did not possess that blessed grace. I said, 'I have taken Christ as my Sanctifier. I just claim it by faith. The altar sanctifies the gift,' etc. But I had never had a real funeral.

"Under ordinary preaching I felt fairly comfortable, and could stand to all the tests put to the congregation. But under the searchlight of the ministry of such men as David B. Updegraff or Dr. Dougan Clark, I would feel keenly conscious of a shortage in my experience. Again and again have I rushed from the meeting into the woods or open country, by day or by night, to weep and cry to God for hours. I really reached a state of conviction, even after I had preached for years, when the wretchedness and anguish of my heart were often inconceivable. My suffering under conviction for inbred sin greatly surpassed anything I endured when an awakened sinner. I had been in the ministry for ten years and, incongruous and presumptuous as it may seem, I had dreamed of places of prominence and honor in my church. To give up my reputation and renounce my ambition for place, and die out completely to what might be said or thought about me, seemed more than I could possibly do.

"But the Holy Ghost had 'harpooned' me, and I found no rest, day nor night, until I gave up entirely. I went on my face before God and lay prostrate before Him, crying for deliverance from the 'old man.' I longed for human sympathy. I remembered ministers who I thought could help me, but no help came. It was the darkest day I ever saw. After hours of agony I began to be filled with a sense of sinking, sinking, and it seemed as if I was dying. Then I began to say, 'Yes,' to the Lord. 'Yes! Yes! Amen! Amen!' The past, present and future, all the known and all the unknown, my reputation, my all, went into God's lap. I gladly consented to be deposed from the ministry. One of the things that the Holy Ghost brought before me at that time was my future attitude toward the distinctive views of our Society—the Quaker Church. Would I follow Him if it led me contrary to my previous religious teaching? I little knew then what was implied or what it would cost me to make this consecration, but I said 'Yes.' I 'died hard,' but I 'died sure.'

"At last there began to creep into my soul a tranquil feeling, a holy hush, a death-like stillness, a sweet, placid '*second* rest.' I had let go, and He had embraced me in His arms. Eight hours later the conscious filling came, and from that hour I had convictions of certainty. 'The old man' was 'put off,' 'the body of sin' was 'destroyed,' 'the old leaven' was 'purged out,' 'the flesh' was 'cut away,' 'the son of the bondwoman' was 'excommunicated,' 'the carnal mind' was 'crucified,' and I was dead indeed unto sin. He did it. No credit belongs to me. The Holy Ghost came in, cleansed the temple, spread the table, and I took supper with the Father, Son, and Holy Ghost that very day. He settled all my difficulties, expelled all my doubts, metamorphosed my duties into delights, dazzled my head with glory and filled my heart with dancing.

"I am deeply regretful that for years after this I sometimes grieved the Spirit by permitting myself to worry, thus allowing friction and worry to come in. Instead of relying entirely upon the Holy Ghost, I was betrayed into a rigid, severe life. I was marvelously preserved from sin, but lacked the sweetness and juice and absolute freedom from care that the Holy Ghost wishes to maintain in His wholly sanctified people. I lost much of the kernel of the *experience* fighting for the *doctrine.*

"A few years since[1] the Holy Ghost taught me more perfectly how to cast and keep all my care on Him, for 'He careth for you.' I took my hands off of men, whether friends or foes; off of my experience, my circumstances, my interests, myself; off of everything and everybody. I am leaning upon the arm of my Beloved. No more irksome tasks, no more 'toiling and rowing,' no more worry, fret or friction! Never a 'hot box'! He is no more *'Baali'* (Master), but *'Ishi'* (my Husband). Hallelujah!"

---

[1] This was written about 1897.

CHAPTER III

EARLY ASSIGNMENTS

It beautifully balances Seth Rees's testimony to the grace of Christian holiness to be able to state that Hulda Rees, too, about this time, received her Pentecost. If the unusual evangelistic team which she and her husband comprised met now with some persecution, it met also, and was marked, with greatly augmented power, and this in turn by far larger success.

A tour of evangelism was made to Kansas and to what was then known as the Indian Territory. Labors of blessed reward were performed among the Modoc, Cherokee and Peoria tribes of Indians.

"I felt clearly called (said Seth Rees) to labor among the Indians. The first tribe that I labored with was the Modoc. 'Steamboat Frank' was the chief, and 'Scarface Charlie' first assistant. The Modoc tribe was simply slaughtered in the bloody conquest of the Black Hills. When war was finished, the remnant of this tribe were loaded into cattle cars like hogs or cattle, and transferred from the Black Hills to the Indian Territory. None of them had heard the Gospel of Christ or had ever been known to shed a tear. In fact for generations emotion, especially weeping, had been suppressed. The Modoc Indian prided himself that he was never known to weep. When the freight cars were unloaded, many of the Indians were dead, and among the dead was 'Steamboat Frank's' little baby. The chief had never wept and had no normal way to express his sorrow, so the course he pursued was to go out into the timber and build him a sort of furnace and sweat himself. It was winter. He sweat himself almost to death, thinking that he might get rid of his sorrow in this manner. Following this he sat on a near-by log, without a stitch of clothing, until he was chilled to the bone. His sorrow remained.

"But when he heard first of the romance of the Gospel, of the love of God in giving His 'only begotten Son,' of how Jesus came into the world and gave His life for a lost race, 'Steamboat Frank,' who had never wept before, shed tears like rain. After he was both saved and sanctified God called him to preach. He changed his name from 'Steamboat Frank' to Frank Modoc. While I could not understand the Modoc language, I could easily catch something of the word-music and eloquence with which Frank preached. He lived, however, only a few years, his use of the hot oven and his exposure to the cold having resulted in tuberculosis.

"Almost the entire remnant of the tribe, numbering only a few hundred, turned to Jesus and to the standards and principles of our glorious Gospel. They held worship in their homes much like our family prayers. They came to my services, men, women and children, as if the Gospel message was the greatest thing they had ever heard. Their papooses were always strapped first to a board and then the board was strapped on the back of the mother. On reaching the church the mothers would remove their papooses and lean them against the wall, baby and all. There must have been an understanding with the little things that there should not be a whimper, regardless of how unpleasant the situation might be, for they were as well-behaved and attentive as anybody in the congregation.

"We then labored among the Cherokees and were greatly blessed; finally among the Peorias and other tribes until we felt we must return to the Kansas Yearly Meeting of Friends."

On one of their inter-tribal journeys they met with an experience that was brimful of thrill and peril. It was the crossing of the Grand River at flood-tide.

"No white man would consider it safe for a moment (says Seth Rees in reporting the event) but we felt we must get over the river to our next tribe at once. So we called on a couple of Indians who were familiar with the stream and consulted them. They offered to swim their horses across if we would follow strictly their course and counsel. We were in an open spring wagon drawn by two horses with which we were not familiar. But we agreed to follow the Indians. Well away from the bank the river poured into the wagon and our horses were forced to swim. We had to climb up and stand on the wagon seat to prevent our being carried away by the stream. The currents were treacherous and it looked more than once as if we would go down to our death. At one point a gesture from one of the Indians barely saved us from disaster. With great joy we at last arrived on the other bank of that greatly swollen river. An evangelist frequently has occasions for shouting and praising his God, and it is too bad we do not do more of it, but I can assure you on this occasion we shouted and praised God. We did more than that—we got on our knees and thanked Him."

On their return from the west Seth and Hulda Rees conducted fruitful meetings at Hopewell and Dublin, Indiana, and at Green Plain and Smithfield, Ohio. The Smithfield revival resulted in their being called to the pastorate of the Friends Meeting at that place. The call was accepted and, in April, 1884, they removed from Indiana to take up the new work. It is of record that "The first winter of their residence in the town the place was shaken with a great revival. The church was built up and the work of God greatly advanced."

In the course of their four-year term of service to the Smithfield meeting there occurred in the lives of these two Friends ministers an event whose repercussions were felt throughout world-wide Quakerism. On the Sunday following the 1886 session of Ohio Yearly Meeting they, together with another minister of the Society, were baptized with water, the rite being administered by two preachers prominent among Friends, A. H. Hussey and David B. Updegraff. The issue thus raised among Quakers on both sides of the Atlantic was that of liberty of conscience on the one hand and strict non-adherence to the ordinances on the other. Discussions were many and lively. The pressure of the issue was such as to force its way conspicuously into the religious press and into the deliberations of the Yearly Meetings. Some acrimony crept in, but in the main the debate went forward on a level of Christian courtesy and mutual respect. Two results definitely crystallized: Ohio Yearly Meeting, sustaining the "good and regular standing" of those who felt led to recognize the ordinances, committed itself to a liberal position; on the other hand a number of Yearly Meetings, by affirming a rigidly conservative view, forbade the use of churches within their jurisdiction for any meetings in which Friends of such questionable loyalty as Seth and Hulda Rees might participate.

Notwithstanding this curtailment of the field of opportunity within their own church, many doors were opened to them for the preaching of "Christ and him crucified" which, after all, was their "meat and drink." It had been pre-arranged with the Smithfield meeting that they should be given three months each year for evangelistic work. This plan permitted them, during the four years it was in effect, to conduct meetings in several states, principally Maryland, New York and Michigan; also to make their first invasion of New England, which was later to become a stage of action for the making of much interesting and spiritually profitable history.

Their presence within the bounds of New England Yearly Meeting raised the "ordinance question." A committee was appointed to wait upon them in remonstrance against their liberal views. But as the snow once saved the Russians from Napoleonic fury so on this occasion it saved the Reeses from ecclesiastical chastisement. A paralyzing snowstorm, such as Whittier describes, prevented the members of the committee from making the journey to the scene of the evangelists' labors. The only member of the group that ever arrived was a good-hearted lady who got so blessed in the services that she forgot all about her mission!

In 1888 the Smithfield pastorate was relinquished for the leadership of the Friends Meeting at Raisin Valley, near Adrian, Michigan. Here Seth Rees and his wife ministered for two years. Of their efforts it was said that "there was the same manifestation of God's grace and favor and power which they had so frequently witnessed in previous work." In the first year a trip of brief duration was made to Iowa, which resulted in the conversion and sanctification of many.

It was in the late 80's and early 90's that Dr. A. B. Simpson, of New York City, was branching out with a distinctive program of evangelism in which were stressed, along with the New Birth and the Baptism with the Holy Spirit, the healing of the body, foreign missions and the premillenial coming of Christ. While never convinced of the accuracy of the movement's slogan-phrase, "The Four-fold Gospel," Seth Rees was deeply impressed by Dr. Simpson's ministry, heartily shared his views on missions and the return of the Lord, largely coincided with him on healing and, in consequence, took a keen interest in the work. While pastors at Raisin Valley he and Mrs. Rees were made president and secretary, respectively, of the Michigan Auxiliary of the Christian Alliance.

In connection with the Smithfield pastorate reference was made to an evangelistic trip to New England. One of the results of contacts made on that trip was the next migration of the Reeses. At the expiration of their second year at Raisin Valley they answered a call to assume spiritual oversight of the Friends Meeting at Portsmouth, R. I. Concerning the visit of some three years before and its outgrowth in the call to leadership at Portsmouth, we have some autobiographical sketches which follow:

"John S. Kimber, who is now a pastor in Los Angeles, and his father lived in Newport, Rhode Island, and heard of me and my ministry. They invited me as their guest. I went into Newport and preached there awhile. About six miles out (Portsmouth) there was an old Quaker Church that had been standing for over two hundred years. George Fox, the father of the Quaker Church, had preached in it in 1672. I was invited there for services. The preaching of holiness was something to which they were not accustomed. Some of these

Quakers were extremely opposed to my coming but the prevailing element wanted me. I went. Their order of service was to gather together and wait in silence for the Spirit to move some one to preach. The congregations were excellent, and God helped me to preach with blessed effect, although we were without a mourner's bench.

"After I had been there and preached as evangelist, I was called as pastor. God was pleased with my ministry. We had the church with its two galleries packed to the limit. Shall I tell you about the church itself? The architecture is beautiful. There is nothing just like it in the United States. Open fireplaces, with beautiful mantles, furnished the heat for us, as they did for George Fox and others of the first Quakers to worship in this country. But the old structure stood in much need of repair. We had the old timbers in the frame bored and tested to see that there was no dry rot in them. We had a new roof put on and the interior redecorated, but we sought to preserve its original appearance and beauty.

"We felt that it was an edifice whose history entitled it to such care as we tried to give it. At one time, in the Revolutionary War, the British red-coats drove the Quakers out and used it as a barracks and its basement as a magazine for the storing of ammunition. The records of the secretary of the local meeting show that for several months, while the British held the church in preparation for an important battle, the members of the meeting were holding their services in private homes. After the battle, known as the Battle of Quaker Hill, the victorious American troops took possession of the meeting house and used it for similar purposes. In cleaning out the cellar our workmen found a number of cannon balls. Some of these were placed in sockets on the mantelpiece over the huge fireplace, preserved as mementos. The battle of Quaker Hill was a costly and decisive one. It is said that 1100 Hessians fell and human blood ran down the hill like a brook."

In the late spring of his first year at Portsmouth Seth Rees launched, under what he was sure was the guidance and providence of God, an enterprise that was destined to be one of the most spiritually fruitful children of his creative and compelling love for Christ and men. The story is not without certain (unintentionally) colorful and dramatic features.

An evening in May—near sunset! A few hundred feet below the parsonage the pastor of the historic church on Quaker Hill is making his way toward a woodland of maples sloping down to the blue waters of Narragansett Bay. His single companion is a devout man of his parish. Now they are pushing their way through the tangled underbrush, bent on exploring the depths of this beautiful bit of forest. They pause. Struck with the charm and fitness of the surroundings, visualizing the whole possible picture, once the ground has been cleared and the trees thinned out, the pastor exclaims: "This would be a fine place for a camp meeting!" The suggestion strikes fire. Two hearts are kindled. They kneel in prayer. Prayer gives way to praise. The stately maples seem to break into singing and the men, not seemingly but actually, into shouting. The shouts are carried, inarticulately, to the parsonage on the hill-top, from whence Mrs. Rees, alarmed, dispatches a messenger to see what is wrong. His discovery: two men filled to overflowing with heaven's joy, so sure are they that a new institution for proclaiming "the fulness of the blessing of the gospel of Christ" has this day been born.

Thus it was that Seth Rees became the human founder and builder of Portsmouth Camp Meeting.

"The next Sunday morning (he says) I announced to the congregation that we were going to have a camp meeting on Quaker Hill and asked for volunteers to turn out on the next holiday, which was the 4th of July, to chop out brush and clean up the grove and make ready for the first camp. This news created a great deal of excitement and some dissatisfaction, but I had the majority with me and the majority grew. Near the center of the grove was a very remarkable stone ledge on which we pitched our first tabernacle—a tent forty feet by sixty. We organized as a committee and applied to the state of Rhode Island as a non-profit stockholders' association. We decided that the camp should be interdenominational and should convene on the last Friday of July. This it has done for over forty years.

"The first camp was opened at 2 p. m., on Friday, July 25, and closed Sunday night, August 3, 1890. It was not large; we could not expect it to be, for our facilities were very limited. We did not have water enough for crowds of camp meeting folk. We had to dig a well, and we struck a stream of the clearest, coldest water that I have ever tasted anywhere. The man who dug the well had recently been saved in my meeting. His name was Isaac (Fish) and the well took its name from him. The first of the twenty-four living tents, which we had rented in Boston, was taken by John Shober Kimber and his wife. Neither of them was sanctified at the time but both of them were sanctified in that first camp. Through all these years they have been true friends."

For more than a quarter of a century Seth Rees remained president of the Portsmouth Camp Meeting Association, rarely missing an annual gathering even when it was necessary to travel hundreds of miles. His rich reward lay in the gladness that came to him as he watched the streams of help and healing that were set flowing down from Quaker Hill to the ends of the earth. To speak thus of the camp's influence is not to flatter the facts with figures of speech; it is to utter the veriest truth. Let one illustration represent many that might be given.

One day, while the camp was in progress, he met a brother who had been in the services for several days and who now appeared, grip in hand, as if he might be leaving. "Brother Moulton," said Seth Rees, as he looked very earnestly into the eyes of his friend who had lately received his "inheritance among them that are sanctified," "I fear you are making a great mistake." The interview was brief but decisive. The impending mistake was not made. Rev. C. O. Moulton remained on the grounds and, in the missionary meeting that followed in a day or so, he and his wife received a call from God to give themselves to missionary work in the West Indies.

Later it was Portsmouth Camp Meeting Association that raised the money to send the Moultons to the islands where, under rare divine grace and guidance, they wrought so nobly and achievingly for Christ. "Exploits in the Tropics," a modest yet thrilling account of the work they were instrumental in founding and forwarding, was published by C. O. Moulton in 1907. Two years later, having laid the foundations of what is now the exceedingly fruitful mission work of the Pilgrim Holiness Church in the Caribbean territory, he passed into the presence of his Lord.

Vitally contributing to such far-reaching effects was the policy adopted by the president of Portsmouth Camp in the selection of his platform personnel. The best was not too good for those who came to sit under the ministries of this Feast of Tabernacles. To it were brought such commanding and anointed figures in the movement for the promotion of holiness as W. B. Godbey, Beverly Carradine, Henry C. Morrison, C. J. Fowler, John Pennington, George D. Watson, Stephen Merritt, John Norberry, Edward F. Walker, Edgar M. Levy, David B. Updegraff, William H. Hoople, Charles Stalker and A. B. Simpson. Mention also should be made of Delia Rees, Seth Rees's sister, a preacher of superior gifts and graces who was associated with her brother in a number of the annual gatherings of the camp. Yes, there were giants in those days, and these were among them.

Said Dr. Carradine of the 1898 camp:

"In all my travels I have never seen a 'freer' camp meeting congregation. Gospel liberty abounded in pulpit and pew, and the responsiveness of the audience was simply delightful."

Said Dr. Morrison of the 1899 camp:

"There were some scenes during this meeting which this pen cannot describe. The Holy Ghost fell in power, and there were demonstrations of His presence that beggar description."

Said Dr. Godbey of the same meeting:

(It) "was a world's wonder for spiritual power and good order, much reminding me of Scottsville and Waco, Texas. The order was the best I ever saw at a large camp. Brother Rees led the embattled host."

Said Dr. Levy:

"We were much moved by the free, gentle, loving spirit everywhere manifest. The unction rested upon the leader, and the solemnity and reverence with which he conducts all the services cannot fail to impress all that this meeting is not for recreation as an end, or for oratory, or for controversy, but for the conversion of sinners and the sanctification of believers. The very collections are like sacraments."

Portsmouth Camp continues to this day, without, however, the large attendance that formerly supported it. It was the joy of the founder to be one of the evangelists at the 1930 gathering, and to participate in the celebration of the Fortieth Anniversary. On the last night, after a sermon by Rev. C. B. Fugett, there were, by a happy coincidence, *forty* persons who responded to the invitation.

It may be added here that on Sunday afternoon, August 6, 1933 (the day on which Seth Rees would have reached the age of seventy-nine), the Portsmouth Camp Meeting Association conducted a Memorial Service. The following ministers were present and spoke: Dr. H. F. Reynolds, Rev. E. G. Anderson, Miss Martha Curry, Miss Elizabeth J. Trout, A. B. Starbuck, Melvin Pratt, Henry Mosher, Claude Roan and C. L. Slater. Rev. A. B. Starbuck, president of the association, was in charge. Eight veteran supporters of the work were present: Edward Macomber, Edward Ailer, Edward Faulkner, Fred Holman, Mrs. L. M. Hedley, Mrs. Jane Dore, Mrs. Carrie Deblois, Mrs. Stephen Dore. Five of them had not missed a camp in the forty-three years. One of the members of this "Old Guard" went back as far as forty-seven years in witnessing to the work of grace wrought in her life under the ministry of the departed founder. Among the ministers Rev. Claude Roan, Superintendent of Ohio Yearly Meeting of Friends, and Rev. Martha Curry, pastor-evangelist, told how, under his faithful, fiery preaching, they were brought into the experience of entire sanctification. Miss Curry remarked on the extraordinary number of preachers and missionaries who had received their call to service under his influence.

CHAPTER IV

CONFLICTS AND CONQUESTS

WHILE Portsmouth camp was being established on a permanent and promising basis in the early 90's, other tasks and ministries evoked Seth Rees's tireless energies and extended his growing influence. For one thing, the local church was on the aggressive. In one report he wrote:

> "The work of the blessed Holy Ghost in saving sinners and sanctifying Christians, moves steadily on. A number who, less than one year since, were far down in sin, are now among the blood-washed, 'whiter than snow,' justified and sanctified, and, although blessedly ignorant of much of the ecclesiasticism of the church, they are safer spiritual guides than unsanctified theologians."

Meanwhile, he and Hulda Rees were in increasing demand as speakers at all-day meetings and conventions in various parts of New England. Among the places visited were Pawtucket, Everett, Fall River, Chelsea, Stoneham, Malden, Amesbury, New Bedford, New London, Boston and Providence. Regularly they were on the program of the monthly "all-days" at Weybossett Street Mission in Providence and Pitt Street Mission in Boston.

At Tiverton, Rhode Island, between their home and Fall River, they helped to reopen a Friends Meeting that had been discontinued. It was a rejuvenation to which were set many seals of providence. In a letter under date of December 22, 1891, written to his spiritual father, Calvin W. Pritchard, who had, for conscience' sake, taken a stand against him in the issue of water baptism, Seth Rees wrote:

> "DEAR BROTHER:—Thee will doubtless be interested to know that, at Tiverton, R. I., where thee preached one Sabbath afternoon when in the east last summer, there is now in progress a most blessed revival of New Testament salvation. Services are held nightly, and all classes are reached.
>
> One wicked sailor opened the stove door and put his pipe and tobacco in the fire before he came to the altar. Another sailor, steeped in sin for more than fifty years, who swore almost constantly when at sea, and was even worse in port, came rushing to the altar and seems wonderfully saved. When told by his companions that he was a fool, he said, 'I wish I had been a fool for fifty years.'
>
> Thee will remember that Tiverton is where the Friends meeting was discontinued and the house closed twelve years since, but re-opened a few Sabbaths before thee was here.
>
> Two years ago the house was offered for sale but thank God He prevented its being sold. We are expecting greater things yet. Pray for us. God bless thee and thy excellent wife.
>
> Thy son in and for the Gospel,
>
> SETH C. REES."

Of the few diaries kept by Seth Rees the earliest is for the year 1892, the last full year of his Portsmouth pastorate. From its pages flash certain intimate disclosures of the life he was living "hid with Christ in God."

January 8: "We have spent this delightful winter day in our little study. This is a most precious spot, made so by the presence of the Lord. We are both fully saved."

January 19: "My faith groweth exceedingly. Praise the Lord!"

February 3: "I have had a blessed time this A. M. in the first chapters of Genesis."

February 9: (Following severe illness) "We are more than conqueror this A. M. Spent the forenoon, both of us, writing sermons."

February 19: (On sudden change in weather) "It is just like spring. Mark Twain says 'New England has weather to loan, to sell, to give away, and more weather to the square inch than any part of America.' I praise the Lord for it all."

March 10: (Following illness of both children and some difficulties in the church) "The cloud of trial and testing which has hung over us for three weeks has burst. Glory! We are the stronger and tougher for the storm. Hallelujah!"

March 19: "We are greatly blessed at morning worship. This is the 19th anniversary of my birth into the Kingdom of God. Sent a little thank-offering to C. W. Pritchard, who was used in my conversion. I keep this day as a day of thanksgiving. Meeting at night in our parlors. Great power. One converted, one seeking the Lord."

April 12: "My soul is delighted with God. Meeting in the evening (convention in Massachusetts town) small and very dry for a Holiness League. I think the holiness people need blessing."

May 3: (At Somerville, Mass.) "I am filled with a consciousness of the nearness of Jesus. We begin a four days' convention. 7:30—I preached. Four seeking holiness, and a grand breaking up among God's people."

May 22: "Trials thick. Glory thicker."

June 28: "In the study praying over a sermon for next Sabbath. I think I have found a starter. Glory to God!"

October 24: "I am watchful unto prayer."

November 22: "It is one of those days when Satan seems to try every fiber of my being but I do have the victory."

December 1: (In the midst of great concern over the failing health of Mrs. Rees) "The storm from hell is unabated. The north winds seem to be fully awake. Glory! Every fiber of my being is the Lord's. The armies of hell are defeated."

January 1 (1893): "This the beginning of another year finds me having outgrown my clothes (spiritually). I am leagues in advance of where I was a year ago."

In the spring of 1893 Seth and Hulda Rees terminated their ministry and residence at Portsmouth, Rhode Island. There followed nearly twelve months of "spreading Scriptural holiness" through an extensive evangelistic itinerary. In Quaker communities they not infrequently encountered opposition to their liberal view of the "ordinances" and their stand on "divine healing." These criticisms notwithstanding, their ministry in its central emphasis was so true to the heart of the Gospel, so Christ-exalting and heaven-owned, that revivals of intense power and, with few exceptions, extraordinary proportions broke out under their leadership. Notable in results were meetings conducted in Philadelphia and Boston; Damascus, Ohio; New Castle, Kokomo, Westfield, Bloomingdale and Bridgeport, Indiana; and in New York City. In the nation's metropolis some outstanding conversions and sanctifications were witnessed in a number of gospel centers—Florence Crittenden Mission, Berachah Home, John Street Methodist Church and the Traveller's Club.

Descriptive of a day in the Florence Crittenden Mission, there is the following journal entry:

February 23, 1893: "We are late into New York. Breakfast on boat. Took elevated up town. Florence Mission at 10. Meet warm greeting. Hulda spoke in the A. M. It was a meeting of great power. A drunken woman and drunken man at the altar, and Mrs. Cramer, (General) U. S. Grant's sister, seeking sanctification. I asked those who desired to be sanctified to stand up. Mrs. Cramer stood. Then I asked those sinners to stand who wished to be converted. The two drunkards stood, the woman an awful case. Then the devil said, 'You will not dare to ask Mrs. Cramer to the altar with that drunken harlot.' I said, 'Yes, I will.' And I did. They both came, and were blessed.

"Here we met Lydia Kenney. Also met Mrs. Dennitt for the first time. She invited us to Mt. Lake Park. S. H. Hadley, of Water Street Mission, was in the meeting. I preached in the afternoon; not less than thirty at the altar. A most wonderful meeting in the Holy Ghost. He did it all. Met Mrs. George M. McKay, wife of a wealthy Wall Street broker. She came to the altar and was wonderfully saved. She had never opened her mouth in public. A Philadelphia Quaker, just out of state's prison, was saved, and Oh! so many wonderful cases."

Seth Rees's fifth pastorate took him outside the regular ministry of his own denomination, though his personal standing remained unchanged. On Sunday, February 18, 1894, he preached his first sermon as minister at the Church of Emmanuel in Providence, Rhode Island. Emmanuel congregation, ecclesiastically independent, was committed to the full gospel of an uttermost Redeemer and to a program of vital evangelism. Here for two and a half years, Seth and Hulda Rees, as co-pastors, witnessed a constant stream of salvation. The work was a "going and growing" concern; its progress brought great delight to its leaders.

Of the many interesting "flashlights" in Seth Rees's diary for '94, two are exceptionally revealing. The first shows that the preacher's life was not all "moonlight and roses" and the second that "times have changed."

April 13: "L. M. came to tea. There was nothing in the house for tea, and we were out of money. Hulda went to Loring's bank and borrowed 35 cents, and sent out and got things; and we praised the Lord together."

May 30: (All-day meeting at Church of Emmanuel) "The grandest day ever witnessed. Stephen Merritt with us all day. He preached about seven hours. (!) House packed all day with people and with the power of God."

Reporting on their first year in Providence, he wrote:

"It is a year since the Master called us to the pastorate of a mission Church and two missions in this city. What a glorious year! Hundreds of drunkards, gamblers, harlots and common sinners, as well as mechanics, bankers, merchants and Church members, have been gloriously saved. It is not our work, it is His. The blessed Holy Ghost is doing it all. During twenty-two years' ministry we have never witnessed a work so widespread, and yet so deep and permanent. Many drunkards have not only been saved from rum, licentiousness and tobacco, but their bloated and diseased bodies have been healed, their faces freed from rum-blossoms, and their wrecked, ruined lives made entirely new. The Holy Ghost has done blessed work among the poor seamen through the sailor's branch, as well as for the sick and homeless through the hospital and free-lodging departments. Our city missionary has been enabled to render some assistance to every case of destitution coming under her notice. Providence, the second city in New England, with all her boasted wealth and culture, has awful slums. But it is very gratifying to know that God is saving and sanctifying wholly many of these poor unfortunate ones."

The year that followed was no less achieving. The church supported from ten to twelve home and foreign missionaries. Its all-day meetings were notable for fine fellowship and thorough-going evangelism. Many were the honored advocates of "Scriptural holiness" who brought to these occasions the benediction of their presence and the appeal of their evangel. Among them were two women of distinction in the cause of the redeeming Christ. One was Mrs. E. M. Whittemore, of New York City, founder of "The Door of Hope" homes for women and girls; the other was Mathilda Atkinson Minthorn, pastor of the Friends Church in Augusta, Maine. Her husband, Dr. Minthorn, was an uncle of Ex-President Hoover. Subsequently to her work in New England Mrs. Minthorn spent many years as a missionary in Alaska.

Early in 1896 the pastor and people of Emmanuel Church brought Dr. Beverly Carradine to the city for a series of meetings. Of this event Dr. Carradine wrote at length in *The Methodist*. He said in part:

"We have had from the beginning to the end a most delightful and gracious time. The night audience became so large that we had to move to an up-town church. On the second Sabbath we moved the second time, and this time to a still larger church, which the Lord as promptly filled.

"One morning a Presbyterian of the 'straitest sect' was sanctified while I was giving an illustration. I have a talk which I have given at comparatively few places, in which I speak of springing up on the waves of doubt, trouble and opposition, and stepping from one to another, and from a high one to a still higher, till perfect victory comes. Several times I have been so carried away with the thought that I am actually rushed into life-like illustration, and on this occasion leaped from the floor to a chair, and from a chair to something higher, and from that to the top of a high upright piano. The Presbyterian gentleman was sanctified while I did this—and in giving his experience afterward said, 'I received the blessing between the time the doctor left the floor and the moment he alighted on top of the piano.'

"Now I trust no one will begin to use pianos and gymnastic feats to spread the truth. I do not depend on such things—but simply feel 'free.'

"There were scenes of such grace and power from day to day that I was carried back to my pastorate at First Church in St. Louis. . . . The meeting at Providence, R. I., will always remain a most gracious memory with me.

"The Rev. S. C. Rees and his wife, with a noble band of sanctified workers, are pushing the work of free and full salvation in great faithfulness and success.

"Brother Rees is a born general and is one of the most inspiring leaders of a religious meeting I ever knew. His prayers always remain in the memory after being heard as gems in happiness of expression and abide in the heart from their unctuous power. They always moved the audience, and brought the sanctified to the shouting point.

"Some of his sayings as he directed the testimony meeting come to my mind. A few people had been rather prolix, and so Brother Rees requested all such that they would 'cut their testimony off at both ends and give us a chunk out of the middle.'

"At another time the audience had been singing with great gusto, 'There's Sunshine in My Soul Today.' Brother Rees cried out, 'Are you sure it is not moonshine?' The speech grew on me as I meditated. I remembered that moonshine is only reflected light. Some people have not the joy and heat of an indwelling light, but they get what is reflected from a meeting, circumstances, or pleasant surroundings."

In Providence, as at Portsmouth, Seth and Hulda Rees found themselves abundantly supplied with opportunities for outside ministry. All-day meetings and conventions called for their services, which were invariably, time and health permitting, gladly rendered. Stamford and Putnam in Connecticut, North Attleboro, Lowell and Boston in Massachusetts, North Scituate in Rhode Island—at these and many other places they labored, in company with such well known leaders of the movement for the promotion of holiness in New England as H. N. Brown, J. N. Short, Daniel Steele, Deacon Morse and C. J. Fowler. At North Scituate a fourteen-year-old girl yielded herself to the Lord Christ. The girl became Rev. Lura Horton Ingler, who for thirty-five years has been a soul-winning minister of the gospel.

Autumn of 1896 brought another change in the field of Seth Rees's ministry. It was a change dictated, he felt, by clear guidance from God. The Emmanuel pulpit was relinquished for the work of evangelism. This vocation, in which husband and wife were almost inseparable, was both intensive and extensive. In the winter of '96 and the spring of '97 remarkably fruitful revivals were conducted in Mt. Pleasant and Cincinnati, Ohio; Pittsburgh and Wayne, Pa.; Baltimore, Md.; Albia and Paton, Iowa; Washington, D. C.; and Portsmouth, Va. Following the camp meeting season of '97 their itinerary included notable campaigns in Wilmington, Del., Knoxville, Tenn., Gloucester, N. J., Chester, Pa., and Brooklyn, N. Y.

And then came the shadows!

Failing health now began to curtail the amazingly successful ministry of Seth Rees's helpmeet—"Hulda, the Pentecostal Prophetess." The Brooklyn campaign was virtually the last in which she labored with accustomed freedom and vigor. While speaking at a mid-winter convention (1898) in Providence, she contracted a severe cold. Despite the rapidity of her subsequent physical decline, she continued to preach. Nor did she cease until even the extraordinary faith and courage which were hers could no longer surmount the limitations of a collapsed body. An account of her last days and her marvelously triumphant translation appears in some sketches and diary-notes by her husband:

"When she sickened, I did everything that man could do for the return of her health. In an almost dying condition of consumption, she was, in answer to prayer, gloriously healed at the Portsmouth Camp Ground. I shall never attempt to explain it, but within a year from her definite healing she was attacked by tuberculosis in another form. It was a terrific blow to us.

"When I saw that hope was gone, that she could not live, I took her back to her old home where she was born and reared (Cherry Grove, Ind.). She lived only a few weeks, but during this time she was filled with prophecy and praise. One day as she sat in a lounging chair, I said to her, 'My dear, is it all true—these things that we have preached?' 'Yes, yes,' she answered, 'we have not put it strong enough! It is all true, and more!' "

To a minister whom she had known for years, she said: "The glory holds!"

"At 3:15 this afternoon (reads a diary entry) Hulda had an awful spell of suffering, which lasted an hour and fifteen minutes, except for a brief intermission, in which she sang the hymns, 'I shall be like Him' and

'The cross is not greater than His grace,
The cloud cannot hide His blessed face;
I am satisfied to know
That with Jesus here below
I shall conquer every foe.'

The glory of the Lord filled the room."

The night before she was translated she attempted to sing,

"Fear not, I am with thee;
Oh, be not dismayed,
For I am thy God,
I will still give thee aid."

She could only whisper the words, however, and her husband read the entire hymn to her.

The end came June 3, 1898. Calmly, struggle-free, she fell asleep—in Jesus!

"She had made every arrangement for her funeral (wrote Seth Rees) and had requested no flowers nor eulogies. Cherry Grove Meeting House was crowded for the funeral. The preacher in charge, Rev. John Pennington carrying out her wishes, gave a simple Gospel message to the living, after which several seekers gathered about the casket in penitence and tears. It was the strangest funeral, but the most glorious one, that the people in that section ever witnessed. This noble woman stood loyally by my side for more than twenty years in preaching the message of full salvation, and went Home with a vast number of souls following her who were saved and sanctified under her ministry."

But the grace that supports the dying is not less adequate—sometimes not less striking—than the grace which sustains the living. This chapter in the warrior's life may be fittingly closed with a pen-picture, by Mrs. E. E. Williams, which appeared in *The Christian Standard* shortly after Hulda Rees went to be with her Lord.

"'The Pentecostal Prophetess,' the beloved Hulda Rees, has just closed her eyes upon earthly scenes, and opened them upon heavenly glory. Her faithful, loving, almost adoring husband, Seth C. Rees, has stood by her side until the last. She had been everything to him that a true wife and friend could be to the one beloved above all others, and now she was gone! Oh, 'tis true her end had been one scene of holy triumph from the moment it was known that this was to be her last sickness. Even when the pain had been the most excruciating, the presence of God had made the death chamber glorious! Her last words had been words that can never be forgotten by those who heard them. . . . Not for our life would we rob God of the glory that is his due in the death (?) of this his saint.

"But at the same time we are beholding another scene. In the church she had loved in life a company of 'Friends' were gathered that Sabbath day, waiting for some one to bring to them the Word of Life. In the home below lay the body of one who had often stood in that place to tell the old, old story, but nevermore would they hear it from her lips until they heard it in the form of the 'New Song,' which only the redeemed can sing. And their hearts are sad, and silence fills the room. But they are not to be left that day without a preacher. Could *she* speak, she would not have it so! A man arises, a voice is heard, and the message of God is delivered by the husband of the woman who lies ready for the grave, but as yet unburied in the old home below!

"Oh, amazing grace! Oh, transcendent power! Sufficient in death, aye, and sufficient in life as well! Shall we magnify the grace that sustained Hulda Rees in dying and forget the grace that undergirded her husband afresh for the battle? No, never! Keep on publishing the 'dying testimonies of the saved,' but don't forget to tell the living that he is able to keep, even in the most trying time that mortals ever know!"

CHAPTER V

THE WARRIOR AT LARGE

"Soon after the translation of my precious wife, I entered upon a most vigorous campaign against sin and Satan in camp meeting work. Having stood for several days on the borderline of eternity, where I could almost see the burnished walls and glittering towers and shining gates and streets of gold and where, as it seemed to me, I could almost hear the gates swing on their hinges, I felt that I must take up the work alone, which had been planned for both of us.

"I have drawn my sword and thrown away the scabbard, and I turn from the grave with the feeling that I would rather preach myself to death in three months, and go up the steeps of light as she did, than to be an ordinary Christian and attain the age of Methusaleh."

Such was the spirit in which this Quaker of Westfield entered upon a new epoch of life and ministry.

Alone, yet not alone!

From the point of view of his natural powers and their development, he was marching into his prime. A quarter of a century in pastorate and itineracy had deepened him as a man of God and seasoned him as a minister of the Gospel. In the order of providence he was stepping out upon a platform as broad as the nation, his inimitable "singing" voice, Celtic through and through, "ringing out the glory of the Lord" from Cape Cod to the Golden Gate. It was a voice virile with all the confidence of ambassadorial appointment, vibrant with all the chastened joyousness of triumphant living.

How did he look? Ask any of his old friends! Large of body, high of forehead, with brown eyes flashingly expressive, his strong, open countenance framed by dark hair roached back on the left side and a Van Dyke beard, he stood, without effort at distinctiveness, a commanding figure with a commanding message. Many are his old acquaintances and spiritual children who remember him very vividly as he then appeared, his dynamic pulpit deliverances flung white-hot at his audiences, with the assistance of animated gestures by those singularly small, tapering hands. The total impression created was that of manliness and Godliness fused into electric effectiveness by the fire of the Holy Ghost.

To make these comments seem less subjective, if not less partisan, it may not be improper to quote from two eminent leaders with whom Seth Rees was at this time associated.

"As for Brother Rees," wrote Dr. Beverly Carradine, "I know of no man in the Holiness ranks today who preaches more convincingly and unctuously than himself. I do most heartily commend him to my friends and brethren, North and South, who desire a man filled with the Holy Ghost, and one who is as good a leader as he is a preacher."

"Rev. Seth C. Rees," declared Dr. H. C. Morrison, "is a mighty man of God. Large physically, large mentally, but largest spiritually, he makes an unexcelled leader of the hosts at a great holiness camp-meeting. He is a man of much prayer and strong faith. He puts God to the test and things come to pass. There is no man in all the holiness movement who preaches with more fervent power, and direct effect on the masses, than Seth C. Rees."

These were the halcyon days of that unique American institution of summer evangelism—the camp meeting. To the thousands who frequented such sacred retreats as Mountain Lake Park, Md., Salvation Park (Cincinnati), Ohio, Douglass, Mass., Pitman Grove and Ocean Grove, N. J., the presence and preaching of the "Quaker Evangelist"—sometimes billed as the "Earthquaker"—were hailed as an event, even though, as was often the case, the jolts received were not a little uncomfortable. As an illustration of the latter point one thinks of the case of Margaret Bottome, to whose marked experience of full sanctification his ministry made a convicting contribution. It was at Mountain Lake Park. This cultured lady, prominently associated with *The Christian Herald* and "The King's Daughters," underwent a deep and drastic experience of being "crucified with Christ." So much so that when her sister, who had accompanied her to the camp, remonstrated with her for giving as much as $50 in the offering, she replied, "Why not, my dear? Haven't I many times paid more than that for a *dress,* and this was for my *shroud!*"

For three successive summers he preached to the throngs at Pitman Grove. For its value as a contribution to the historic record of American camp meetings, as well as for its fitness in this memoir, the following report of one of his Pitman visits is entitled to a place here:

"Pitman Grove (he wrote) is sixteen miles out of Philadelphia on the West Jersey and Seashore Railroad. It is one of the largest camps in the East. Seven hundred cottages, electrically lighted streets and avenues, pure, wholesome water and a beautiful grove, make it a charming 'city of the woods.' The plan of the 'city' is unique. The auditorium, said to accommodate four thousand, is in the center of a circle from which twelve beautiful avenues radiate like spokes from the hub of a wheel. There are four hotels on the camp ground. On one side of the camp is an enclosed tabernacle, large enough to hold five or six hundred persons. Here Brother E. L. Hyde holds two wonderful meetings each day at 5:30 a. m. and at 6 p. m. In these meetings there is a constant stream of salvation. On the opposite side of the camp is Lizzie Smith's Holiness Temple (capacity three hundred) where Sister Smith conducts meetings on the definite line of holiness at 1:30 and 6 p. m. Sisters Boyd, Stewart and others assist Sister Smith to keep a red-hot holiness meeting in operation. It is a feast of fat things and a perpetual banquet.

"It was our privilege to preach at the auditorium to large and appreciative audiences for nine days. We received the hearty cooperation of the Association. God poured out His Spirit and we have reason to believe that much was accomplished that appears only in the record on high. Here it was our privilege to listen to Bishops Grant and Fitzgerald and be much blessed under their ministry. Brother Ballard, who is president of the Association, is also first vice-president of the camp at Ocean Grove, which fact made it necessary for him to be absent much of the time.

"We have fallen in love with the Pitman brethren and do not hesitate to say that we have not met so large a body of ministers in any part of the land who seem so devout and pious as the ministers of the New Jersey Conference. They are not all in the experience of holiness, but the number who oppose the doctrine is comparatively small.

"Among the number who were sanctified one afternoon was a girl eighteen years of age, whose striking face under the sanctifying power shone like electricity. We afterwards learned that she was a class leader with thirty in her class. Another young woman had been seeking earnestly for some time, when she arose with a positive testimony and said she had given everything to the Lord. We were impressed to say, 'Do you believe He accepts you now?' After a moment's hesitation a light played on her face and with a half-suppressed smile she modestly said in a subdued tone, 'He can't turn me away!' The effect was wonderful. Glory filled her soul and the fire ran all through the audience. People shouted and wept and laughed and danced before the Lord. Pitman Grove is the only place we ever preached where they shouted us entirely off our feet and forced us to stop before we were through the sermon.

"At the last service the holiness band from Sister Smith's temple marched down to the auditorium and around the circle and up on the great platform to greet us, singing as they marched, our favorite hymn, 'Never Alone.' We thought to slip away to the train unnoticed, but when we arrived at the station a large company had assembled who sang and waved their handkerchiefs until our train was out of sight. May God keep the dear Pitman saints until Jesus comes!"

A sermon delivered at Pitman Grove on the afternoon of August 12, 1898, elicited the following remarks, which appeared, it seems, in the *Pitman Messenger:*

"Evangelist Seth C. Rees preached one of the best sermons preached at the camp meeting this year, from the words found in Colossians 2:7, 'Rooted and built up in him, and stablished in the faith, as ye have been taught, abounding therein with thanksgiving.'

"It was a marvellous effort. God was with him, and the Holy Ghost working through him gloriously helped the people, winning their sympathy, and best of all, reaching their hearts. Brother Rees was very unjustly criticised during the first part of the meeting, but the mighty power of the Holy Ghost soon swept away the unchristian criticism, and turned the hearts of critics as well as friends into the great channel of salvation, which day by day spread throughout the camp meeting. The immense congregations which attended all the services held by him proved the influence he swayed over the people. May this God-fearing, Holy Ghost-filled, wonderfully-saved man, under the blessing of God, be spared many years to go up and down this sin-scarred world, scattering the fire of the Holy Spirit and preaching this very same gospel of truth and salvation that he preached at Pitman Grove this year."

By Bishop Fitzgerald, of the Methodist Episcopal Church, Seth Rees was invited to deliver the closing sermon of the Ocean Grove, N. J., Camp, in 1898. Reports of the occasion appeared in a number of periodicals.

"The last preaching service on Monday evening," ran one account, was one of the most extraordinary of the entire series. The preacher, a quiet, wide-awake, but unobtrusive looking gentleman of Quaker parentage and training, turned out on the platform to be a perfect cyclone of sacred eloquence. Of all the orators who have honored Ocean Grove with their presence, not a single one captured his audience so quickly, and carried the thousands hanging on his words so completely away. Rev. Seth C. Rees, the Quaker evangelist, was the man.

"His sermon last night, aside from gesticulation and some extravagant form of illustration, was incandescent with spiritual power. Laughter over odd comparisons, tears when the speaker touched the tender and pathetic cords of the heart, and genuine Methodist shouting, swept like a whirlwind over the vast congregation.

"His theme was Christianity symbolized by springing water and affluent rivers, indicating the amplitude of God's provision to save and sanctify 'whosoever will.' "

Real as are life's losses, they are no more so than its compensations. Two things were requisitioned by providence to relieve the loneliness and supplement the loss that Seth Rees experienced in the death of his wife and companion in the ministry. The first was the stepping to his side, in the fall of 1898, of a preacher-son. For such an hour of comradeship and comfort, not to mention other things, Byron J. Rees had "come to the kingdom." Born, like his father, at Westfield; clearly converted at the age of five; led into the experience of a clean heart at Douglass (Mass.) Camp Meeting while in his fifteenth year; recorded a minister in the Society of Friends at eighteen; educated at Brown University, Oak Grove Seminary (Maine) and Earlham College, Richmond, Ind., he became, late in '98, the subject of the following announcement in *The Christian Standard:*

"He has attended camp meetings at Portsmouth, Richmond, Cadmen's Neck, Pitman Grove, Douglass and Mt. Lake Park. He has been active in all-day meetings and in various holiness work. He compiled a sketch of his mother's (Hulda A. Rees) life. He has furnished articles to several holiness papers. He is the author of 'Hallelujahs from Portsmouth, Nos. 2 and 3.' He is the author also of 'Christlikeness,' about to be issued by the Christian Standard Co., of Philadelphia.

"His ministry is developing into one of extraordinary power. His faithful and gifted mother having been taken from his father's side in evangelistic work, he will now accompany him in all his work. He is still a young man, but graciously endowed with unusual ministerial and evangelistic gifts. This is God's order to go out two by two. May God abundantly bless father and son, so that their last days may be their best."

That God did "abundantly bless" them is evident from some preserved accounts of their meetings, which appeared in the religious and secular press. Conventions and camp meetings of remarkable power and effectiveness were conducted in Lowell, Mass., Meridian, Miss., Knoxville, Tenn., Normal, Ill., Allentown, Pa., Wilmore, Ky., Chicago, Ill., Kansas City, Mo., and Denver, Colorado Springs, Pueblo and Cripple Creek in Colorado.

The meeting at Normal was sponsored by the late Rev. M. L. Haney in whose heaven-hallowed home the evangelists were entertained. Among the fruits of their labors in this place was the reclamation of Cecil Troxel, who later found the "way of holiness" under the ministry of Dr. H. C. Morrison and then went out to China to engage in the monumental mission work with which his name has been so intimately connected for more than a score of years.

At Chicago there were more than "500 souls at the altar as definite seekers in twelve days." "To say that there were 100 converted on the last Sunday alone would be a conservative estimate." The convention at Lowell, too, was conspicuous for displays of spiritual vitality and redeeming grace. A quotation from a report by the evangelists reveals how glad their own hearts were made:

"What a glorious convention this has been! What prayers have ascended! What hymns have swelled and rolled! What testimonies have flashed and sparkled! Imprisoned souls have leaped into liberty, and the crown of Christ has sparkled and shown with fresh glory."

Of this meeting Rev. A. B. Riggs, the pastor, wrote:

"Truly we have seen great displays of God's power beyond all our past victories, which have been so great. We thought we never should see again a greater work. Some of the leaders say it has been the greatest work God has ever done for this people."

The second event which brought a benign compensation to Seth Rees's bereft life was his marriage, in November of 1899, to Frida Marie Stromberg, of Providence, Rhode Island. The officiating minister was Rev. John Pennington, a dear friend from boyhood days who had succeeded the groom as pastor of the Church of Emmanuel and who now, at the age of eighty-eight, lingers in the mellow light of life's setting sun. Feeble of body but alert of mind, he graciously contributes the first chapter of Part II of this memoir.

Like the "Pentecostal Prophetess" who had preceded her in the office of helpmeet, Frida Rees was a devoted worker who was by no means unaccustomed to the public phases of Christian ministry. Immediately she took her place on the platform by the side of her husband. Their wedding trip took them, after a stop at the nation's capital, to Laurens, South Carolina, for what proved to be one of the foremost revivals that ever blessed that locality.

"The meeting began (wrote Seth Rees) in a tent that will seat one thousand people, pitched in the block next to the court house. This tent was almost full at the first service, and the power of God fell upon the people until about fifty came rushing to the altar. Many and wonderful were the victories of that first night. The second day of the meeting another tent that would hold five hundred was pitched, and the two were joined so that we could preach to both congregations. The colored people were permitted to occupy a part of the smaller tent.

"When a long double altar was packed to its utmost capacity, and people were on their faces in both aisles, I announced that Mrs. Rees would go into the other tent and conduct an altar service. The colored people gathered around her and fell on their faces, and a number were saved and sanctified. The county sheriff was gloriously converted and stood and said: 'Fellow citizens, I have been drinking whisky for years. I have tried to stop it, and could not. But now God has saved me, I want to say to the men with whom I have been drinking that you should come down here to this altar and let God save you.'

"Many came, and one testified the next day, 'I have drunk whisky for twenty years, but God has saved me and taken away all desire for it,' and, pointing to a little woman near him who was bathed in tears of joy, he said, 'Here is the little woman who has stuck to me all these years. I hired a man to work in my place today, that I might come to this meeting and tell it.'

"Mrs. Rees preached one morning to a large congregation, and about fifty fell at the altar, and such victory and power I have not seen in twenty years."

Approximately one thousand souls sought some definite blessing in the Laurens campaign!

CHAPTER VI

SOME NOTABLE OFFENSIVES

INCIDENT to his work as an evangelist were certain interests in which Seth Rees had begun, meanwhile, to figure with increasing influence. In 1897 he had united with Rev. Martin Wells Knapp in setting up a simple, non-sectarian organization known as the "International Holiness Union and Prayer League." "We felt," he says in some personal sketches, "we could not continue to cooperate with the modernism that was then appearing and the lack of spirituality that was general in the churches to which we belonged." The doctrinal basis of membership in the Union, while centering in Christ as Saviour and Sanctifier, included two commitments that narrowed its appeal and stamped the movement as radical; commitments, namely, to the "premillenial" view of Christ's return and "divine healing."

For five years Seth Rees served as president of the Union, other officers being Rev. M. W. Knapp, Vice-president; Rev. W. N. Hirst, Secretary; Rev. Byron J. Rees, Corresponding Secretary; Rev. C. W. Ruth, Treasurer. "Extensive revival was carried on . . . resulting in the formation of many missions, churches, rescue homes, and camp meetings, as well as the sending out of missionaries to many foreign lands. Bible Schools were established and papers published at Greensboro, North Carolina, Owosso, Michigan, and other places."

It was this movement, gradually taking on a denominational aspect, that developed ultimately into the "Pilgrim Holiness Church." Known after 1905 as the "International Apostolic Holiness Union and Churches," it was, in 1913, reorganized as the "International Apostolic Holiness Church." It assumed its present name and structure in 1922 on the occasion of the union with it of the "Pilgrim Church." Of the last mentioned development we shall have more to record in connection with a later period of Seth Rees's life.

His association with Rev. M. W. Knapp was at once manifold in activity and mutual in understanding. It represented a unity of spiritual purpose and passion produced by the fusion of different backgrounds and dissimilar personalities. Both men were insistent on honoring the Holy Ghost as "the executive of the Godhead" in this dispensation of the Church; the "things of the Spirit" were magnified because they were felt to be so tremendously real and so immensely important.

Near the close of the century, after ten years of service as a monthly periodical dedicated to the promotion of holiness and evangelism, *The Revivalist,* edited by Rev. M. W. Knapp, made its appearance as a weekly, with Seth Rees as Associate Editor. "A Full Salvation Journal" was the sub-title that floated at its masthead. Into thousands of homes it went every week, carrying, in addition to the contributed articles, the best work of its consecrated staff—the Knapp editorials, the Godbey Sunday School expositions and question drawers, the Rees sermons and supplementary editorials. Then, as now, it was published at Cincinnati.

It was not with a view of cultivating and displaying any literary gifts that this editorial post was accepted, but rather that the good news of the Grace of God, which he delighted to preach, might have a more extensive and effective proclamation. Seth Rees had come to believe vigorously that the Gospel from the pulpit should be supplemented by the Gospel in print. He had been confirmed in this conviction by the reception that was given to his first book, THE IDEAL PENTECOSTAL CHURCH. Of this effect, and of the circumstances connected with the writing of it, he says:

> "While holding meetings in Cincinnati, Ohio, in November, 1896, I was led to preach on the qualities and characteristics of the Pentecostal Church. Fire fell out of the skies, and about twenty-five persons hurried to the altar. The blessed Holy Spirit suggested that I was not getting the Pentecostal message to the people fast enough, and that I ought to write it and send it forth. Night after night He awakened me and talked with me about it while others were asleep. When my mind was clear that it was God's will, the book was written and offered to the public without apology. God has blessed it to many thousands, and will, I humbly believe, to thousands more."

"Written in clear, nervous English," to use the terms of a reviewer in the *Religious Telescope,* it "glows throughout with the evangelical fervor of its author." That the "Ideal Pentecostal Church" is a "Clean Church," that it is a "Powerful Church," that it is a "Witnessing Church," that it is a "Liberal Church," that it is a "Joyful Church," and that it is always a "Missionary Church"—these are some of the propositions which the book declares and develops. It was published in 1897.

Camp meeting history, too, was being made at this time. In 1898 steps were taken by M. W. Knapp that resulted in the setting up of a large union camp in the suburbs of Cincinnati. It was called "Salvation Park." Not a few readers of these pages will remember it as a place of extraordinary influence in the converting of sinners, the sanctifying of believers and the calling of Christian workers and ministers. They recall to this day the anointed labors of Brothers Knapp, Godbey, Fergerson, Stalker, Weigle, Cornell, Kulp, Pennington, Rees, and others.

Of Indian Springs Camp, in Georgia, where he ministered in 1900, Seth Rees wrote:

> "It is one of the most delightful holiness camps in all the Southland. . . . Those who planted it ten years ago, and maintain it today, have had much to encounter, but they are God's brave, true men, and he has lifted up a standard against their enemies. They are now reaping glorious results, and the increase of their labor will yet be more abundant. Brother G. W. Matthews is one of the strongest and most fearless men we have ever met in the South. His devoted wife is a strong preacher, and would grace any pulpit in the land. Brothers Dodge, Tilman, Christian, Benson, and others, are pushing the war against sin in Georgia, and the Holiness movement is taking on more rugged qualities than for years.
>
> "The meeting was not what we would call a 'sweep' for God, though every day was an advance, and souls were saved and sanctified at almost all of the services. I think that more than one hundred professed to get into the light in ten days, and

some of them were ministers. Two ministers swept into the experience of sanctification in one service. To say that we fell in love with these large-hearted, ardent-spirited Southerners is to speak very moderately. Dr. E. M. Bounds, of Washington, Ga., preached some very strong sermons on regeneration, prayer and the Lord's coming."

Soon after the birth of their first child, Paul, late in 1900, Seth and Frida Rees removed from Providence to Chicago.

The following year found Seth Rees and a number of his brethren promoting two conventions which for publicity, intensity and fertility remain to this day as memorable occasions. The first was held in Chicago, the second in Boston. Two of Chicago's most commodious Methodist churches, First Church and Metropolitan, were secured for the services in that city, one being used for day meetings and the other to accommodate the great throngs at night. Those on the platform of the convention included Rev. John Norberry, Rev. E. A. Fergerson, Rev. T. C. Hodgin, Rev. "Bud" Robinson; also Rev. E. L. Harvey and Rev. D. M. Farson, Chicago business men whose zeal for the winning of the lost to Christ had led them into the ministry, and "Andy" Dolbow, a marvellously redeemed drunkard who still, at nearly ninety, abides in the church militant as a monument of saving grace.

Conversions and sanctifications were witnessed not by scores but by hundreds. The daily papers took notice and their reporters, both by serious news items and by comic caricatures, gave many columns of free advertising. The revival took on such proportions that its services, which were scheduled to cover ten days, lasted for seventy-five days. Not less than 2200 seekers were dealt with at the altar. Many preachers were in attendance, one of whom, Rev. F. Arthur Ingler, received the inspiration for writing "The Pearly White City," a song with which his name has been widely associated.

"Chicago (wrote Seth Rees after the meeting had been in progress for several weeks) is being visited by one of the most stirring, old-fashioned revivals known to it for many years. About thirteen hundred souls have been at the altar seeking God, besides many who have been saved in the congregation or in their homes or places of business. Thirty-five were forward as seekers last night and fifty-one the night before, and so the work goes on, and we see no end to it.

"Since the close of the convention in the heart of the city, which lasted two weeks, the evening meetings are held in a large Methodist Church on the North Side. Among those who have been saved have been saloon-keepers, policemen, drunkards, lawyers, bartenders, thieves, harlots, church members, preachers and all sorts; men and women of note and position as well as bums and soaks. The great reformer at the head of the anti-cigarette crusade, Lucy Page Gaston, fell at the altar and was gloriously sanctified.

"Brothers Dolbow and Norberry are still with us, and may remain some weeks. We are just about to open two Rescue Homes, one for women and one for men. A part of the furnishings have already been donated by those who desire to assist in this slum movement. 'Thy right hand, O Lord, is become glorious in power; Thy right hand hath dashed in pieces the enemy.' All glory to His name forever!"

The Boston Convention, held in the winter of 1901, was even more spectacular. It was conducted under the auspices of the Portsmouth Camp Meeting Association, whose practice it was to have annually a mid-winter gathering of the workers and witnesses for holiness in and about Providence and Boston. As president of the Association, Seth Rees counted largely on the able support of a noble sanctified layman, Mr. F. M. Messenger, then a prominent mill man of North Grosvenordale, Connecticut. To this earnest gentleman of affairs fell mainly the business management of the Boston meeting. Park Street Church was secured. It was in the neighborhood of high revival traditions, for "Brimstone Corner" was there, where Charles G. Finney preached so mightily on the terrors of God's holy law. Brothers Robinson, Farson, Harvey, Fergerson and others were brought from points distant; local leaders included John Norberry, of North Grosvenordale, and John Pennington, of Providence. The battle waxed hot, as Seth Rees's account of it shows.

"We hired the church at $25 a day, paid in advance. We began to open fire in a place where there had been no fire for years—not a conversion, I was told, for many years. From the very first service of the convention people began seeking the Lord. I think it was on the fourth night that, after I had finished preaching, I stepped up on the cushioned front seat to make the altar call. The officials of the church were angry. They called me to meet with them, accusing me of desecrating with my unholy feet the cushion of that first pew, which was used at the time of their observance of the Lord's supper. The shoutings and demonstrations of our people, too, must cease.

"Well, the newspaper reporters wanted to know what we were going to do. I replied that we did not know. I sent out nine committees of two and two to comb Boston for a place in which to finish the convention. Finally the committees reported that Mechanics Hall, the largest auditorium in the city, was the only place available that was big enough. The reporters were present; everything was tense because of our predicament. The Hall rented for $400 a day, plus $20 a day for police protection. I did not see how we could pay such a price. In a few hours the manager of the Hall, having been interviewed a second or third time, came to our hotel and told us that for the next five days we could have the use of it for $1500, with $100 extra for police protection. After praying about the matter, we decided to accept his offer.

"We paid nothing for advertising; the newspapers took care of that on their own initiative. Eighteen of us did not look like much on a platform that would accommodate two hundred. In front of us were 9900 chairs. The first service was at night. There were perhaps 7000 present. The altar was well filled with seekers. As they got victory some of them 'shouted uproariously,' as Godbey would say. Hundreds sought and found God in the next few days. I can hardly go to Boston without somebody telling me that he was saved in that meeting.

"Some Harvard students got to coming. They were curious and were out for fun. Some of them created a disturbance one night about the time of the altar service, so we decided to make inquiry rooms out of the quarters that the Hall provided just back of the platform. A few of them, as fake seekers, made their way to the inquiry room. They didn't know what they were getting into. Several of them, surrounded by genuine seekers and godly workers and an atmosphere of prayer, were saved. That put an end to the faking of the university students.

"Sunday we seemed to have Boston at our feet. No one attempted to disturb or molest in any way. The fires of God swept the crowds of people. The altars would not hold the seekers. Such weeping! And then such shouting! I got to see what I wanted. After we had paid the Hall rent and our board bill and other expenses, we left the city with money in our pockets and a little to give away. One man gave us a check for a thousand dollars."

It seems only fair to state that in these conventions there were some emotional excesses that proved, in the case of certain persons, to be more fleshly than spiritual. It was not long until the "Farson and Harvey" element, which eventually headed up in the "Burning Bush" movement, carried matters to such extremes as to forfeit Seth Rees's confidence with respect to the soundness and safety of their leadership. A separation became imperative.

Between the two conventions that have been described there passed a busy summer of camp meeting travel and labor. Soon after the laying of the cornerstone for the Tabernacle on the "Mount of Blessings" at Cincinnati, in April, on which occasion he delivered a special sermon from the text, "Holiness becometh thine house, O Lord, forever," the Rees trio—father, mother and infant son, Paul—made a trip to the far West. Revivals that netted many blessed accessions to the Church of the living God were conducted at Salem and Newburg, Ore. This trip was a forerunner of many that were due to follow in later years.

As the year 1901 drew to a close, death broke into the circle of Seth Rees's intimate comrades in ministry, removing his much-beloved brother, Martin Wells Knapp.

"A prince in Israel has fallen (he wrote), a general has died at the front. He was at the firing line, and was found with the armor on.

"Our precious brother Martin Wells Knapp, has been promoted from the Church militant (fighting) to the Church triumphant. They killed him, but God took him.

"As for us, we are greatly bereaved; we are in sorrow beyond expression, but in joy eternal. I want to die like that myself—with the harness on, and hugging the reproach that comes to a true soldier. I doubt if any man living stood closer to him than I have for the past three years, and I know he was truly 'a good man, and full of the Holy Ghost and faith.' He would have me be careful to say that all that he was, he was by the grace of God."

This promoted leader had left no inconsiderable monument in the form of a full-gospel center—Bible School, Rescue Home, Tabernacle, publishing plant—on the "Mount of Blessings," at Cincinnati. For three years Seth Rees continued in active relation to the work. At the close of this period he severed his connection.

Other tasks were calling.

CHAPTER VII

IN TRENCH AND ON FIELD

LATE in 1901 Seth Rees had heard a Macedonian call. Answering it, he was guided to open a home for the salvaging of the lives of prostitute girls and women. Later, maternity cases were accepted. The simple name given to the institution was "Rest Cottage." The work prospered and bore excellent fruit. It was far more than a venture in social uplift and adjustment; from the first it was distinctly evangelistic, its objective being primarily the spiritual regeneration of those to whom it ministered, and secondarily their social rehabilitation for lives of respectability and usefulness.

"The many friends of our rescue work in Chicago (he writes in October, 1901) will be glad to know that our Home for girls is now open. The dedication took place on Saturday night. The power and glory of God came down like a cloud, and filled all the house. Some souls were saved, some were sanctified, and others were definitely called to the work. God certainly put His seal upon it in a very marked way. The work in the slums is being signally blessed. The poverty and suffering in certain districts is simply appalling. But souls are being saved in the attics and hovels and jails and grimy lanes and where the gospel would never reach but for this 'highway-and-hedge' movement.

"The work seems overwhelming. Winter is coming on, and our missionaries could use almost any quantity of cast-off clothing of all sizes. Think of a mother, with a mother's heart, being forced to put her children to bed before night to keep them from freezing—with scant covering, zero weather, and not a pound of coal in the house! May the compassionate Saviour help us to reach and to save the largest number of souls possible!"

Thus there was added to the multiplying activities of the evangelist and author and administrator a piece of work that was destined to grow far beyond any conception or purpose that attached to its beginnings. For the vision quickly expanded to wider horizons. Soon a "Rest Cottage" was opened at Providence, R. I., and another at Greensboro, N. C., and still another at Elkhart, Ind. In 1903 the fifth home announced open doors in Kansas City, Mo. Homes six, seven, eight and nine followed in Columbus, Ohio, South McAlester, Okla., Pilot Point, Tex., and Colorado Springs, Colo., respectively. A few years later the tenth institution established under his direct supervision was put in operation in Los Angeles. Each of these shelters, assisted usually by the ministries of some evangelistic church or city mission, became a spiritual workshop in which life's "broken earthenware" was mended by the matchless Hand of the Master-Potter.

Outstanding across the years has been the work of the homes at Columbus, Kansas City and Pilot Point. The first has been, for a number of years, under the efficient control of the Society of Friends, and the other two in the care of the Church of the Nazarene. Approximately fifteen hundred girls have passed through the Kansas City home, and about the same number through Pilot Point, while at Columbus they have handled nearly two thousand cases. This is exclusive of babies and children who have been sheltered. Prominently associated with these havens of help, and with the success that has attended them, have been the wise direction and untiring devotion of three noble matrons: Evangeline Reams at Columbus, Lue Miller Roberts at Kansas City and Minnie Lindberg Roberts at Pilot Point. Mrs. Lue Miller Roberts is the only surviving member of this splendid trio. She is now associated with her husband, Rev. J. P. Roberts, in carrying on the work at Pilot Point.

Peculiar difficulties beset the work in the early history of Kansas City "Rest Cottage." Concerning these and kindred matters Mrs. Roberts recalls:

"Brother Rees maintained a very deep interest and very close direction of the work in those trying days, and became an arm of great strength to its establishment. There were times, however, when he became greatly exercised as to the wisdom of continuing. He returned time and again to take the matter up in private consultation and in public services, seeking clear light as to whether he should close the home or further establish it.

"Outstanding in this ministry was one particular afternoon when he took for his text, 'Let us go into the next town.' He presented the difficulties and then gave the people the opportunity to express themselves. It was one of the most beautiful services that it was ever my privilege to be in. Much over a thousand dollars was subscribed to erect a building, and a lot was given. It is very gratifying to know that the money subscribed was later turned to the purchase of property, and all of the assets provided on that wonderful day are still going on in the work for which it was given.

"Many difficulties continued to be the heritage of the home, and at two different times laws were passed especially to greatly hinder the progress of the work. On one of these occasions Brother Rees was used of the Lord to be such a tower of strength. After attending a camp meeting at Hutchinson, Kansas, he called a number of his friends and associates to prayer. As he came to my name he said, 'Lord, we do not know what awaits Sister Miller in Kansas City, but whatever it is, help her.' The following day I was placed under arrest and needed so much the help he prayed God I would have. He immediately sent me a check when apprised of my difficulty, and advised me that if there was further need, to let him know. It was always his great joy that deliverance came as often as the difficulties. His personal contribution to my life has been of no small moment, and the strength of his wonderful personality to press forward in the midst of conflicts made a very worthy example to follow. May God bless his memory."

The work in Chicago included, in addition to Rest Cottage, the pastorate of the Austin Tabernacle, extensive missionary service in the slums, open air meetings and a mission hall on State Street. On the staff of workers, at various times, were Anna Hallgren (Whitworth), Anna Anderson (Hines), Elmina Canaday, Catherine Stephenson (Stalker), Jennie Stromberg (Hodgin), and numbers of others. They were a daring and dauntless group, filled with Christ's constraining love.

As director of slum and rescue activities, Seth Rees was exceedingly careful about his choice of workers.

"It was more difficult (he says) to secure competent matrons and capable assistants than it was to get money with which to carry on. I refused to have anybody who was not wholly sanctified and on fire for God. Our workers had to be courageous. They had to go into dives and saloons at the midnight hour, into dark alleys and filthy tenements. They have been known to go where a policeman did not dare to go. We had no one more courageous than Jennie Stromberg, now the wife of Rev. G. Arnold Hodgin. She feared nothing, it seemed. I knew her to go into dives where she was met with the threat of revolvers. She was defied to move another step. But she was there to rescue some girl and she would not be denied."

The city mission work of those days has a shining trophy in the person of Rev. Carl H. Dauel, evangelist. He writes:

"In my Christian experience no minister has meant more to me, or been a greater blessing in my life, than Brother Rees. It was on December 11, 1903, in Chicago, while I was 'tending bar at 404 Wells St., in the Chicago Music Hall, that workers from the Rest Cottage, which Brother Rees was superintending, came into the saloon and brought me the message of salvation. After six days of awful conviction I went to the mission Brother Rees had charge of, 499 State St., and under the preaching of Sister Hodgin (then Sister Stromberg) I was gloriously saved.

"It was at this time that I came into personal touch with Brother Rees. He instructed, helped and encouraged me in the things of God, until I became established in holiness. The following year, at his advice, I entered God's Bible School at Cincinnati. In later years he was my beloved pastor and, at the time of his death, was my General Superintendent and highly esteemed friend."

As a minister Carl Dauel has been "a flame of fire." He has been superintendent of five city missions, notably Fifth Street Mission, in Los Angeles, where annually hundreds of men and women sought and found the Saviour. He has conducted nearly two hundred revivals and pastored four churches. A number of men now in the ministry were converted through his fiery preaching.

What with the care of these growing activities among the neglected, and the responsibilities belonging to his place as president of the Apostolic Union, Seth Rees might have been diverted from the work of direct evangelism. But he was not. He kept the vision. He forgot not his own calling. He majored in the field to which he felt especially commissioned and for which, under divine blessing, he had demonstrated an eminent fitness. During the years from 1900 to 1908, while, as we have seen, some secondary interests were being formed and fostered, he was conducting meetings from one end of the land to the other. Unceasingly did he press upon the needy multitudes the claims and offers of an uttermost Redeemer. For a number of years, it is true, he made it a rule to condition his acceptance of an evangelistic call on the privilege of devoting one service to the cause of rescue missions.

In 1902 a series of meetings was held in Greensboro, North Carolina, which was notable not alone for its immediate fruitage but perhaps even more for the impetus it gave to the promotion of holiness throughout a large surrounding territory. An interesting memorandum on this campaign is furnished by Mr. M. L. Hollady, of Greensboro:

"In June of this year (1933), thirty-one years ago, Brother Seth C. Rees came to Greensboro, N. C., to hold a revival. He was accompanied by John S. Kimber, Charles Weigle and a number of local ministers from this state. At that time I had never even seen a picture of Brother Rees. I knew of Byron Rees and had in mind that it was he who was to be the leading evangelist in this meeting. So naturally I was looking for a much younger man. I was seated on the platform with several ministers. When it came to the time of preaching, I saw a man who looked as though he might be near fifty years of age, weighing two hundred and fifty pounds, walk slowly to the front of the rostrum, with an open Bible in his left hand. He paused for some seconds, then announced his text, Acts 2:12, placing special emphasis on the question, 'What meaneth this?'

"In a few minutes it seemed to me that his very soul was being lifted from the earth. I was not sure that his powerful body might not follow. I leaned over and whispered to Brother Arnold Hodgin, inquiring who this great preacher was, and he said, 'Why, it is Seth Rees!' I was satisfied.

"The meeting was largely attended. I remember one man from the mountains who walked one hundred and twenty-five miles to get to the services. He said he was amply repaid for the trip. Many of the leading citizens of Greensboro came out to hear the great man of God preach. Among them were some lawyers. One very prominent Presbyterian lawyer remarked to me that never before had he listened to such powerful sermons. Judge Bynum, now deceased, came often.

"I remember asking my dear friend, J. L. Crouse, who about a year ago went to heaven, to go with me to the tent. After two or three services had been held he said one evening that he would go. On that very night he received the Baptism with the Holy Ghost. I never had to ask him to go to a holiness meeting again as long as he lived. He became an ardent supporter of the work.

"Beginning with the first service, the meeting throughout was a great success. Many who were converted and sanctified in that meeting are still in the work of the Lord. And many have been called to their reward and are now in the presence of their Lord, together with their spiritual father, Brother Rees."

It should be added that the J. L. Crouse of whom Mr. Hollady speaks, was a building contractor who, over a period of thirty years, exerted most remarkably a layman's influence in the cause of "righteousness and true holiness." He was a rare and radiant spirit.

In 1903 Seth Rees was called to conduct a revival at Peniel, Texas, the seat of Peniel Holiness College. A marvelous outpouring of the Spirit of God resulted. One who was present says:

"The oldest inhabitants of Peniel still date everything back to 'the Rees meeting.' Will Huff had expressed the feeling that they *must* have Brother Seth C. Rees for a meeting. With the endorsement of the president, Dr. A. M. Hills, and with Dr. J. S. Hill, of Greenville, backing him financially, the arrangements were made.

"The meeting was wonderful almost from the beginning. The school buildings were in the center of the campus, the dwellings built around them. As we went to church it seemed we could hear praying from every house. For three days Brother Rees could not even read his text, much less preach. There were altar services all around.

"The up-stairs rooms in our home were filled with students. Over our heads in the living room we heard boys praying! Above us in the dining room, boys praying! Over the kitchen it sounded like two boys had a chair each, raising it as high as they could and bringing it down with all their might, and praying as loud as they could. One fine young man, of fine family, after standing through several altar-calls with face like wax, went forward. He could get nowhere. Finally he had to get Brother Rees to go with him to the woods where he could tell it all out. It was a very small matter, but it was wrong. He got beautifully saved. To a friend he said, 'Anybody can get saved who *wants* to!' His face was aglow.

"I don't think we ever knew how many were saved or sanctified during those days. We did not 'number Israel.' At that Great Day numbers will greet that great warrior, in gratitude for that great meeting."

In 1905 meetings were conducted in Chicago, Philadelphia, Portsmouth, R. I., Salt Lake, Ky., Mt. Sterling and Columbus, Ohio, Hutchinson, Kan., Thomas, Okla., Moville, Iowa, and Greensboro and Asheville, N. C. Of the work in the last mentioned place, Seth Rees wrote:

"The battle of Asheville was a great triumph. Every inch of ground was contested by the enemy, and it was a stiff fight, but the victory was sweeping. The mountain preachers and workers had gathered from all that mountain district to attend this great annual feast. From the first the altar was crowded with weeping penitents, and often two or three altars were full. It is most refreshing to see these mountaineers seek God. They seem to know no better than to roll up their sleeves and go in with all their might. No less than three hundred were at the altar, and a larger proportion of them 'got through' than is often the case.

"Our Rescue Home and the brave little missionaries are doing noble work there. It was my privilege to accompany them to the County Jail where I preached to four murderers. Two of them had received their sentence to 'hang until dead.' One has a strange feeling when he knows he is preaching to those who must soon stand in the presence of God. It was in this jail that one of our mountain preachers lay for eighty days after he was saved, straightening up his past life."

Shortly after this report was written, a tent, which he had provided for the use of these mountain preachers, was burned with all its equipment, and a young man, on duty as a night watchman, was shot and painfully injured. Strong opposition had been aroused among the liquor and secret order forces. The revivals that had occurred in a number of centers had proved to be hard on certain lines of business! But martyr stuff, like martyr blood, is spiritually germinant. Evidence of this lies in a letter kindly written to the author by Rev. R. L. Maness, of Harrisville, West Virginia, who, as one of the pioneer preachers of those days, is conversant with the facts connected with the destruction of the tent and who, as recently as 1933, has visited the scene of the burning. He writes:

"I began my ministry doing evangelistic work in the tent that was burned. Hundreds of souls were saved and sanctified. Then I turned the tent over to Rev. A. T. Pounders, and he took it near Canton, N. C., and was holding a great revival in it on New Found Creek. The night it was burned he had had a great service. Many were saved and sanctified. The young man who was on guard had fixed himself a place to sleep. He was awakened by the ruffians who shot him in one leg, pulled down the tent, piled it up, took the oil that was used for lights and poured it on the pile, then set it all on fire.

"The young man was called to preach, went into the work, and has led many to Christ. A new church building was put up near the spot where the tent was burned. There is a very flourishing church there now. As the result of this persecution revivals broke out all over that mountain section, and many are faithful to this day who got victory in those days.

"Your father was a wonderful blessing to me and thousands of others."

Reference has been made to Seth Rees's deep interest in literature that was definitely interpretive and promotive of the truth of a full salvation through our Lord Jesus Christ.

"The only way (he wrote) for us to keep fiery and juicy is to be progressive, to be missionary in spirit and scatter the fire. There are a great many ways of doing this, and one of the ways that have been especially impressed upon me in the last few years, is scattering holiness literature at home and abroad, especially on the very needy fields. We have about nine thousand missionaries representing about thirty million professed Christians, and there is a great cry for good full-salvation literature."

It was in keeping with this conviction that, following the publication of THE IDEAL PENTECOSTAL CHURCH, he had sent forth two volumes of sermons: FIRE FROM HEAVEN, in 1899, and THE HOLY WAR, in 1904. To these contributions the year 1905 witnessed two additions. The first was the launching of a paper under the title, *Full Gospel and Rescue Journal,* while the second was the putting out of a fourth book, very different in type from its predecessors. *The Journal* was a sixteen-page monthly, with Rev. John Pennington as Associate Editor. It was unqualifiedly committed to aggressive evangelism and missions. It carried, each month, a sermon by the editor. Letters received from all parts of the world bore witness to the blessing it ministered during the five years of its life. MIRACLES IN THE SLUMS was the title of the book that appeared almost simultaneously with the first issue of *The Journal.* A thrilling chronicle of "deeds done for Christ," it had a wide sale. The stranger-than-fiction stories of twice-born men and women were at once tragic and triumphant across its pages. "It reveals," said one publisher, "the power of the gospel to reach the hardest cases and records many modern miracles in rescue work never before made public."

A quotation from *The Journal* for October, 1906, shows its editor in battle abroad and in trial at home:

"The Rocky Mountain division of our Army, led by William H. Lee and his devoted wife, went into battle in Colorado Springs, August 10th. On account of sickness at home I did not reach them until the 17th. At every service we attended the altar was thronged with seekers for pardon or purity, and many blessed victories were scored. It was most gratifying to me to know that the public men and officials of Colorado Springs have confidence in the leaders of the Holiness Movement there. While we are never to compromise for the favor of the world, it is worth something to have their confidence.

"The last Sunday of the camp was a red letter day. The crowds came, the day was perfect. The power fell and hell was defeated. In the afternoon I preached on 'The Power of the Gospel in the Slums,' and took an offering for the Rocky Mountain Rescue Home amounting in cash and pledges to thirteen hundred thirty-seven dollars and twenty cents.

"I was there only two days and preached five times. The camp closed in a blaze of glory, and I flew back to my sick darling. Little Russell has been sick thirty-two days with typhoid fever, but God has restored him to us. How can we ever praise Him enough?"

By this tender reference we are reminded that the Rees family, in Chicago, had been growing. Russell was born in 1903, and two years later a royal welcome was given to Evangeline, of whom, in the years to come, her father was to speak affectionately as his "only daughter."

Humor occasionally bubbled up through Seth Rees's references to the meetings in which he participated. In the following instance it is mixed with a bit of irony:

"Pilgrim Hall on Court Street (Brooklyn, N. Y.) was secured at twenty dollars a day, and on December 7th we opened the battle against sin and unrighteousness. No victories are obtained in a great center like Brooklyn without an awful protest. But God was with us and stood by us when we preached, and gave victory in every service.

"The whole city of Brooklyn was not 'Greatly Stirred.' There were no 'Sun Bursts,' 'Falling Stars' or 'Moral Earthquakes.' Long Island did not 'Swing Like a Hammock,' East River was not choked up, the saloons were not 'All Closed' and the devil was not destroyed. But I humbly believe that many souls wept their way to the Cross and were gloriously saved. From the first, seekers were at the altar, from three to fifteen at almost every service. I have read so many exaggerated reports of meetings that I sometimes think I will never report another. And yet I know all the true saints are glad to hear of the conversion of sinners, sanctification of believers and the healing of the sick.

"Our old friend and tried warrior, 'Captain' Charles T. Potter, of Norwich, Conn., was with us in the fulness of the blessing. What a luxury to be yoked up with a man who never suffers defeat!"

And here is his description of an event that occurred on the side while a powerful revival was in progress in Indianapolis:

"The pastor of a Congregational Church who had once known God, but who had backslidden by compromising, was put under such conviction that he went before his congregation and confessed his condition. On Sunday night his wife came to our altar and was gloriously saved. He was not at the service. When she came home and broke the good news to him, he never rested until God saved his soul. It was about midnight when the light broke into his hungry heart. That was a night of great rejoicing at the parsonage.

"But the next day he said, 'I want the Holy Ghost; I will never stop until I am sanctified.' In the afternoon he called on us at the Claypool Hotel. We very soon got down to pray. When we had prayed around to him, he broke down, and his groans, sobs and cries created a sensation not common in the

Claypool. But the preacher grew more and more in earnest, and his cries rang out through the hotel corridors, until there was a knock at the door. On opening the door a gentleman said, 'I am the officer for the Claypool. What is the matter? Is some one sick?' I said, 'No, we are only praying, and a man is getting blessed. Do you not pray?' To which he answered in great confusion, 'Yes, yes! Excuse me!' I said, 'Brother, if you will pray right, you will get blessed too.' He bowed and scraped, and away he went, but all this never confused the preacher. He went through and received the Holy Ghost. He will never forget Room 871 in the Claypool."

CHAPTER VIII

A NEW BASE OF OPERATIONS

For Seth Rees and his family 1908 was an eventful year. It witnessed their removal from Chicago, and their journey, by easy stages, to the Golden West.

The year opened with the evangelist in full stride. During its first quarter fruitful meetings were held in Russiaville and Dublin, Ind., Pueblo, Colo., and Belleville and Humbolt, Kan. A remarkable thing occurred at Dublin.

"It was during this convention (he says) that an unfortunate man in Chicago, an ex-convict, a hopeless drunkard, fell under such awful conviction that he went from Englewood to my office in Austin, a distance of a dozen miles or more, to get me to pray with him. He had never met me, but had heard that I was a friend to the hopeless, and that I understood such cases as his. To his disappointment my secretary told him that I was out of the city. He had been all over the country but did not seem to know where Dublin, Ind., was. But he was not discouraged. He found a map, looked up the location, learned that it was two hundred and thirty-five miles from Chicago, and that the round trip would cost him about $10.

"He wanted God. He must find some one who could help him. He had ten hard-earned dollars in his pocket but was told it was folly to go so far to 'see a man.' He was told that 'he could find God anywhere.' 'Yes,' said he, 'but I must have help.' Sitting in the Pacific Garden Mission, at nine o'clock at night, debating this question in his mind, he suddenly reached a decision. Fifty minutes later, when the train pulled out of the

Dearborn Street Station, he was on board with a round trip ticket in his hand.

"At four o'clock next morning he was in Indianapolis, where he had to wait three hours for a Dublin train. When he struck the railroad platform at Dublin, he inquired where the evangelists stopped. At nine o'clock he fell on the floor in my room, and with sobs and groans told his heart-rending story. Such a scene! Such a picture of the wreckage and ruin of a life of sin! Were we ever moved more deeply? Shall we ever forget it?

"Within an hour God wonderfully saved him, and all that crushing load of a thousand tons rolled off his soul. What a light came into his face! What hope sprang up in his heart! He stayed all day, went to church and testified, and returned to Chicago that night. He had been four years and seven months in prison. But here on the bed-room floor he found what he so longed for. Here was a fallen, hopeless man who was not after a sandwich, a mug of coffee or a night's lodging. He wanted God, paid his own way and left with the feeling that it was the greatest investment of his life."

Of the Belleville, Kansas, revival he wrote:

"The meeting at Belleville was certainly a favored time. In some respects it was quite unique. Some who attended the services were above the average in intelligence and education. Others were ignorant beyond anything we have met in the slums. Young married women were at the altar who could not read, and do not know their own age. One lady, who was saved in the meeting, has a family of several children. She can neither read nor tell the time of day by clock. She does not know the exact age of her children. When asked the age of her little boy, she answered, 'Don't know; he was born in 'tater diggin time.' Though she could not read the time on the dial of a clock, she could read her 'title clear' to a mansion in the sky!"

In the spring a trip was made that harked back, in some of its features at least, to the days of '49.

"We were led (says Seth Rees) to consider seriously the matter of making an overland gospel trip to the Rocky Mountains. We laid it before Brother and Sister Hodgin, who are both ministers, and invited them to join us in the trip. After prayer and deliberation we decided to make preparations. We purchased a span of good young horses and the running gear of a wagon. Arnold Hodgin, who is a carpenter as well as a preacher, built a commodious wagon box, or schooner, and on the 20th of April at 5:45 a. m. we started on this long journey.

"We started from Hutchinson, Kan., where my family had spent some weeks and where Brother Hodgin was teaching in the Bible School. The saints were all up by the dawning of the day and gave us a hearty godspeed. We carried a stock of holiness books and copies of the *Full Gospel Journal*. We not only talked and preached salvation on the way, but put *Journals* in the mail boxes and the homes and hotels where we stopped.

"We usually slept in the wagon and a small tent (eight of us in all), but sometimes we found saints who took us under cover and gave us a warm welcome. At Stafford, Kan., we preached in the Friends Meeting House. At Haviland we stayed over Sabbath, preaching, morning and evening, to large and appreciative audiences in the Friends Church. Souls were seeking God. The same was true at Fowler, Kan. At Kismet, Kan., a new town only three months old, we held a nine-day camp meeting. God greatly blessed the services. The hotel manager and his wife were both saved and sanctified.

"The trip was not without testings and trials, but God gave victory over them all. We were held up by storms and bad roads, and finally a sick horse. But after a couple of days we bought another horse and went on, leading the sick one. After so many long stretches of unfenced and unbroken prairie, sometimes fifteen or twenty miles between ranch houses, and a vast territory without a tree or a twig to break the monotony, our hearts were made glad when one afternoon about three o'clock we observed the dim outline of the Rocky Mountains piled up against the blue sky. They were one hundred miles away and more, but they seemed like old friends and greatly relieved our tired eyes.

"The next day they grew quite plain but were still three days' journey in the distance. Our first view of Pike's Peak was like catching a glimpse of an old acquaintance. We have admired this old mountain for many years, and have approached it from all sides in all kinds of weather, but we never beheld it in greater glory than at this time. Like full salvation, it impresses us more profoundly every time we look it over. And on the camp ground, at Colorado Springs, at the foot of this old mountain king, I settled my little family in tents for the summer."

After a summer of intensive camp meeting work in the East and Middle West he returned to Colorado Springs. The Rees tent was folded up and the family entrained for Southern California. Pasadena was chosen as the place of residence. It was destined to become for Seth Rees, throughout the remainder of his life, the "Crown City" of the world. Of all places he regarded it as the fairest and best. Here, in 1909, his family was completed in the birth of Seth Cook, Jr. Here his children received their education. Here his voice was heard across fifteen years of pastoral ministry. Here his life—personality, preaching, prayers—made such impact upon student life as to register itself in inspiration and benediction around the world. Here, for a quarter of a century, was Home. And here, when that quarter-century had run its busy course, he lay down and fell asleep in Jesus.

From his new home-base Seth Rees continued aggressive operations in his unrelenting battle for God and righteousness. Extensive evangelistic travels filled the next three years. Of the many campaigns conducted we have memoranda on only three or four.

To do the work of an evangelist a certain toughness of fiber is necessary, as the following bears witness:

"Contrary to our regular practice, we accepted an invitation to hold a meeting at Ulysses, Kan., without asking any questions.

"The brother who wrote us said that it was off the railroad, but did not say how far it was.

"We naturally suppcsed that it was a place of from two to five thousand people.

"We were instructed to come to Hartland, from which point we would be conveyed across the country to Ulysses. We were also instructed that there was only one train in the twenty-four hours that stopped at Hartland, and that was at midnight; and that if there was no one to meet us, to go to the 'Scott's Hotel' and wait until morning.

"Wife, little Russell and I boarded a train at Hutchinson, two hundred miles east of Hartland. After a couple of hours' ride a gentleman introduced himself as presiding elder in the M. E. Church for all this southwest Kansas; he said he had heard me preach ten years ago at the Wichita camp. He gave me a few pointers which set me thinking. He said there were about thirty people in Hartland and possibly fifty or sixty in Ulysses, and that it was thirty miles over the plains. I wondered if there would be a hotel bus to meet us.

"At 12:45 midnight the whistle blew and the porter shouted 'Hartland!' When they dropped us in the buffalo grass we saw only two men. We asked one of them where the 'Scott's Hotel' was. He looked amazed and said: 'I don't know'; the other one said: 'Yes I can show you. Come this way.' He led us out a way and, pointing across the raw prairie, said: 'You see that light? That's it.'

"It looked to be a long ways off. In crossing the railroad little Russell fell and struck his head on the steel rail. Quite a severe cut it was, too. We held our eyes on the light which grew a little brighter as we advanced.

"When we reached the little prairie cottage we banged on the door several times without response. Finally an old man from upstairs shouted, 'Come in!' We entered and found our way upstairs as best we could, and after a time the old man found a match and lighted a little old lamp and let us into a little room with a bed, but without mirror, water or bowl and pitcher or anything of the kind. Tired and hungry we retired three in a bed and slept a little.

"Next morning early a man pushed a back door open and came bolting his way through our room. It was his only way of escape.

"We arose, dressed, went downstairs and asked where we could bathe our face and hands. The old grey-bearded agnostic said: 'You have to go into the east room.' The east room was a little filthy shed where we found a rusty iron basin and a bar of laundry soap. The breakfast we touched lightly, and were glad to be off across the plains. After we had driven a few miles the driver said: 'If you want a drink of water you had better get it here for it is ten miles to the next house.' We began to think that we had found the 'West,' no mistake. He said: 'We will have eight miles of bad road and then it will be better.' Well, they were long miles and when they were behind us we felt that we were far from home. Twenty miles more to drive over the unbroken and much of it unfenced prairie! *Not a tree or bush or shrub of any kind* did we see in the thirty miles. We passed a school house with the doors and windows out, where twenty years ago there was a city of two thousand people. There is not a soul within miles of there and the only trace of the city is this old hull of a school house.

"We passed another place where there had been a town of fifteen hundred people, but today there is not so much as an old school house left.

"Ulysses was once a live town of twelve or fifteen hundred people. Today there are sixty people and the only three buildings of any size are the court house, school house and hotel. We were entertained in the hotel and the wolves came into the dooryard and howled furiously at night. We saw them in the day time without going far from the house. One man has trapped about four hundred in one winter.

"This county (Grant) is twenty-four miles square and there is not a church house of any kind in the county.

"Our meetings were held in the school house. People came from the country until we had about one hundred in attendance. Some drove ten or twelve miles to the meeting at night. Some few were saved and sanctified, six being the most that were at the altar at any one time.

"The brother who called us to this meeting is a young holiness preacher with a wife and baby. They are both frail and have come to this dry country hoping that the high altitude may be beneficial to their health. They live on an unfenced claim in a one-room sod house, 12x16 feet. Not a trace of any other building on the claim. He is full of fire and energy, and preaches whenever he is able, without salary. He never takes a public offering for himself.

"Such men will outshine the sun in the City of Gold. How we love these frontier saints! God bless them forever."

How true it is that the results of Christian evangelism are not statistically reportable or predictable! A quarter of a century later one is able to say that among the few who entered into a gracious religious experience in the Ulysses meeting was Rev. R. S. Winans, who was later guided to missionary work in South America. For years he has been a devoted and capable representative of the Church of the Nazarene in Peru.

"In Seattle, Washington (wrote Seth Rees, referring to a revival campaign in the Church of the Nazarene), walking from the church to my room one afternoon, a young man overtook me and, putting his arms around me, said, 'Brother Rees, it was by reading one of your books that I was saved. I was very wicked and went to church only three times in seven years. I worked Sundays the same as any other day. One Sunday I was hauling posts and my mother got up on the load to ride a ways. She had one of your books in her hand and accidentally dropped it down among the posts. She knew me to be such a hot-headed fellow that she was afraid to ask me to get it. So when I unloaded, I found it and laid it up in my room. The next day I was sick in bed and wanted something to read, and the only thing in reach was that book. I read your sermon on the text, "God hath chosen the weak things," etc., and it put me under such conviction that I went and told my mother that I was going to be a Christian. I gave my heart to God and He saved me. Three days later He sanctified me, and now I am superintending a mission down in Kennydale, about twelve miles out of Seattle.'

"Well, all this rolled off his tongue so fast that it almost took my breath, but we stopped right on the street and praised the Lord together. Glory!"

In San Francisco, while preaching in the Victory Theater, he accompanied mission workers to the (in)famous "Barbary Coast," where saloons and dives grew quiet under the cadences of his voice as he proclaimed Christ Jesus the Lord, the Mender of broken lives and the Healer of broken hearts.

In Portland, Oregon, a revival of remarkable power was conducted in association with "Bud" Robinson. Two campaigns were held in Los Angeles, one in the Women's Temple with Rev. Will Huff as co-laborer, the other in the First Church of the Nazarene, Dr. P. F. Bresee, pastor. In the latter meeting his companion in ministry was Rev. I. G. Martin.

"This is a unique gathering (wrote Seth Rees) and the church has had a great victory. I should judge there were some times 2000 people present. The attendance was at least large, and we certainly had a great meeting. I was told that between three and four hundred seekers were at the altar during the two weeks."

CHAPTER IX

BATTLE SCARS AND RE-FORMED LINES

It was now nearly fifteen years since Seth Rees resigned his Providence pastorate to re-enter the evangelistic field. Including the brief interlude of shepherding the flock at Austin Tabernacle, in Chicago, they had been strenuous years, but "full of good fruits." In 1912 the call came to return to the work of a pastor. The University Church of the Nazarene, newly organized at Pasadena, desired his services. Beginning with one hundred and fifty charter members, it was splendidly representative of the growing movement with which he had felt led to identify himself soon after establishing residence in Southern California. The call was accepted.

Nazarene University, from which the local church took its name and on whose campus it worshiped, was a thriving institution of learning presided over by a nobly gifted Christian educator, Dr. H. Orton Wiley. Between pastor and president developed a relationship of affection, understanding, and desire that made for highly effective coordination of purpose and program. It was not long until the University enrolled a student body numbering approximately four hundred and fifty, and the church was able to report a membership of nearly four hundred. A magnificent enterprise was moving forward under the manifest blessing of Almighty God. A cultural and spiritual center was being builded with promise of great, perhaps unprecedented, usefulness. The situation was one to delight angels; by the same token it was one to evoke the "stratagems of the devil," to use Weymouth's phrase.

Probably the most notable event in the four years that these men labored together was the great revival of 1914.

"Brother Wiley and I so perfectly cooperated (wrote Seth Rees) that there was never any occasion for differences between us in any way or manner. We were both groaning for the salvation and sanctification of every student in the school and every member of the church. Such a burden for this rolled in upon many of us that we had, in all, thirteen nights of all-night praying. We prayed for nothing but for a revival. It came.

"About 8:30 one morning the Holy Ghost fell upon the whole fifty acres. In the grade school they could not have any recitations; the boys and girls were weeping and praying and meeting the Lord. Almost at the same hour the same thing was occurring in the class rooms of the high school, the college and the music department. Soon the Divine Influence reached the dormitories. While all this was happening President Wiley was busy in his office, looking forward to the 11 o'clock chapel hour. The pastor of the church was busy at home, a mile from the campus, and did not know anything of what was going on. About an hour before time for chapel Dr. Wiley learned about the marvelous visitation of the Spirit, the influence of which was sweeping the school. Bells were rung and chapel was called early. When I reached the chapel service at 11 o'clock, the auditorium, which held about four hundred, was packed. I think it is safe to say that a hundred people were on their feet, weeping, praying, making confessions, shouting for joy. Such a sight I had never witnessed.

"It was not long until I understood the whole situation; I realized our prayers and groans were being answered openly. The meetings continued day and night for weeks. Some were stretched out on the floor, apparently unconscious, but they never failed to come through with glorious victory. Some of these very persons are leaders in the church today. The influence of the revival reached far beyond our campus. Business men of the community, merchants and bankers, were affected. They were not critical; they had confidence in us. We had been careful, both personally and as a church, to meet our obligations.

"Students who went through that meeting still praise God for it. No human hand could have had much to do with it, for when it began the president was in his office and the pastor was in the parsonage, a mile away. Oh, that such a revival would strike our schools and churches today!"

Other brethren gave equally high appraisal to this epochal outpouring of the Spirit of God. To the *Herald of Holiness* President Wiley sent the following telegram:

"Great revival at Nazarene University! Scenes beggar description! Friday a modern Pentecost meeting broke out. Simultaneously in different departments classes turned into altar services. Students shouted over four hours in chapel and dining-room. Over one hundred saved or sanctified during the day. Attendance large and increasing. Much confession and restitution. Sunday beyond description. Dr. Bresee preached morning and evening. More than fifty at altar. About three hundred seekers at altar during week."

Speaking of the meeting as a whole, Dr. Wiley said, "For depth and power I have never seen its equal." "The revival on at the Nazarene University," declared Rev. W. C. Wilson, cannot be described. I have never witnessed, in all my camp meeting and revival work, such a meeting." "To witness the scenes around the altar of the old chapel," observed Rev. J. P. Coleman, "was like reading a chapter from the history of early Methodism."

One wishes that it were possible to record continuing happy relations between University Church and the institution with which it was identified on the one hand, and the ecclesiastical District of which it was a part on the other hand. Neither statement can be made. His splendid leadership encountering increasing difficulty, Dr. Wiley resigned the presidency. The new administration inaugurated new policies which, in the main, were believed to be unfriendly to the church. By this time there had developed a complex of facts and attitudes in which Seth Rees and University Church were the center of controversy. Certain methods of administering pastoral discipline had been called in question. The pastor, moreover, had stood solidly by the president in withstanding and seeking to correct some teachings in the University which both men believed to be contrary alike to Scripture and to Nazarene doctrine. Differences between brethren had become critical. The story is a long and painful one, the details of which neither the space nor the purpose of this volume will permit.

Events moved to an astonishing climax. On Sunday, February 25, 1917, while the pastor was leading his people in worship, the District Superintendent appeared, requested the privilege of the platform and, this granted, began to read from a document which he drew from his pocket. As he finished, a stunned congregation—the third largest in the denomination—began to realize what had happened. They had been disorganized and dismembered, their official existence as a society declared null and void.

There followed three months in which the ejected church waited for a review and a possible reversal of the District Superintendent's action. Unofficial protests arose from every quarter of the denomination. It fairly may be said that Nazarenes at large did not approve of what was obviously, from the point of view of the makers of Nazarene discipline, an unjustified assumption of ecclesiastical authority. The General Superintendents, excepting one, made a ruling which evidenced their judgment that the intent of the Manual had been exceeded and the spirit of the law violated. Beyond this, however, almost nothing was done. The Southern California District Assembly, which convened two months after the disorganization, did not see fit to re-open the case. While individual members were permitted to apply for admission to other Nazarene churches, University Church was allowed to remain a congregation officially disbanded.

Now it easily would be possible to wax emotional in an extended narrative of the whole deplorable proceedings. The writer of this memoir has no thought of yielding to such an impulse. Seth Rees and those who stood with him, with whatever mistakes they may have made—and it would be folly to claim infallibility for them—

have long since rested their case with a higher tribunal than that of men or movements. It remains, nevertheless, for this biography to lay down a few simple statements of fact.

Let it be said in all fairness, calmly and kindly, Seth Rees did not withdraw from the Church of the Nazarene, nor did he lead any secessionist movement. He and the church which followed his leadership with extraordinary loyalty, were expelled by disorganization on charges that had to do neither with morals or doctrine, and this without a hearing. Whatever the change that was effected in their official status by the ruling of the Board of General Superintendents, it was felt by the pastor and people of University Church that their case was hopeless from the standpoint of the District and its leaders. Out of this conviction arose their decision to organize separately.

Let it be said still further, and still without rancor, that, as regards various phases of the difficulty that climaxed in the expulsion of University Church, misrepresentations were more or less unintentionally sown throughout the country, from which Seth Rees suffered much, even at the hands of old friends. For years he was a figure suspect with certain persons and groups of persons who later had their prejudices either corrected or buried in forgetfulness.

In June, 1917, as the result of events which it has been necessary for this chapter to record, the pastor and people who formerly constituted the University Church organized themselves as an independent unit, the Pilgrim Tabernacle, of Pasadena. To this group and its rapidly expanding circle of interests Seth Rees gave himself in pastoral devotion. He continued so to do until 1925.

For a short time those local churches, in California and Texas, which grouped themselves in sympathy with Pilgrim Tabernacle and in protest against the policies and acts leading to the disorganization, called themselves the "Pentecost-Pilgrim Church." Soon, however, it was deemed best to drop the term "Pentecost." The simple title, "Pilgrim Church," was employed until, in 1922, as related elsewhere, the little organization united with the International Holiness Church to form what is now known as the "Pilgrim Holiness Church."

Seth Rees was nothing if not aggressive. A monthly paper was started, known as *The Pilgrim*. A Bible Training School was set up, offering courses of instruction for grade school children, academy students, prospective Christian workers and, subsequently, for those desiring junior college work. In the school enterprise he was assisted at first by Dr. John Matthews, later by Rev. G. Arnold Hodgin. No one, his wife excepted, knew how many students he personally assisted to make their way through to what he felt was a minimum of preparation for Christian service. While he lay at the point of death he received a letter that was typical of many which were sent to him through the years. It read:

"The day of my graduation has come! Five of the happiest years of my life have been spent in Pilgrim Bible College. Your kindness and generosity have made it possible for me to remain through this year and graduate. . . . My only regret is that you will not be present tonight to give us our diplomas."

If, as pastor of University Church, he had been missionary-minded, Seth Rees was more intensely so in his ministry and leadership at the Tabernacle. It was his devout dream to be pastor of a church that raised more money for missions than it raised for itself. There were several years when that dream was realized. The monthly Sunday night missionary march was a notable feature of the work. From three to four thousand dollars a year for world-wide evangelism was the way the offerings ran. And still he was not satisfied.

Forth from the Tabernacle and the Training School went preachers and missionaries who had caught the "vision splendid," who believed the whole Bible, rejoiced in a Divine Saviour, bore the evidences of cleansed hearts and flamed with the fire of the Holy Spirit. One of these was Rev. Francisco Soltero who, with his capable wife, returned to his native Mexico to establish a most remarkable missionary work. So remarkable indeed has it been, and so close was it to Seth Rees's heart, that some account of it is deserving of a place in this record.

The Solteros left Pasadena in January, 1920. They were given a farewell offering of over $400. A few months later, when a suitable location had been found for the opening of their work, the Tabernacle sent them $600. The Pasadena Pilgrims, says Brother Soltero, "continued to send us monthly amounts to cover our needs, which increased as the workers were increased, until they were sending us regularly $320. This they did for some time before the union of the churches in Cincinnati."

What were the results on the field? In a few months there was a thriving little church in San Luis Potosi, numbering thirty-five members, and a Sunday School of seventy-five. The next year saw the Huasteca section invaded. The gospel worked in power. New missions were established. In 1925 another offensive was launched. It was among the Aztec Indians. These hardy survivors of a noble civilization of the past were astonishingly hungry to know the God Whose saving love and power Christ died to reveal. They were converted by the hundreds. Many of them have been Baptized with the Holy Spirit and become earnest workers.

In the meantime the Solteros were joined by other missionaries from the Pasadena Tabernacle—the True sisters, Nella and Ethel, and Mrs. Rilla Chapman. More devoted and heroic workers never carried the missionary banner of the Christ. In 1927 a Bible School was opened. Native ministers were increasing. Conversions and sanctifications were being witnessed on every field. "The work has progressed," writes Superintendent Soltero, "until now there are more than one thousand members, beside all who are safely in Glory, and perhaps three thousand or more who regularly attend the services in our churches. At present all the work is carried on by native workers."

And this was the work fathered and fostered by Seth Rees and Pilgrim Tabernacle!

"His letters," remarks Brother Soltero, "were always full of courage and alive with hope and possibility, urging us on to greater things for God. How could we help but go forward with a man like him and a church like the one he founded, backing us and praying for us continually? When we wrote him of special burdens and problems, he always took time to answer every detail in full. If he had no stenographer near, he wrote in a clear, bold, long hand. The endings of his letters were tender and touching. They revealed the mighty currents of divine love that surged through his very being." The following are quotations from letters received by Brother Soltero:

> "As to financial conditions, they are not improved at all with us. Your letter distresses me more than I can tell, but there seems to be absolutely nothing we can do. . . . I refuse to be discouraged. I am willing to go on half rations. I am not willing to admit that I am defeated. God is on the throne both here and in all the fields. I am willing to take my place along with the sufferers wherever they may be.
>
> With tender and even sorrowful
> Christian love, I am,
> Your brother,
> SETH C. REES."

> "Yours of January 24th is before me, part of which I had answered, perhaps not in full. Your distress only adds to mine, and I am willing to share with you and all the missionaries in it all, but seem powerless. . . . It looks dark in every direction except straight up; I refuse to be discouraged. . . . Sink or swim, survive

or perish, live or die; as long as I have breath I must preach holiness.

"With Christian love to all the fields, remembering kindly and especially your dear wife and Sister Chapman, as ever,

His and yours,

SETH C. REES."

"Brother and Sister Hodgin are here, and are making such wonderful reports about the work in Mexico that I want to go there at once. I cannot say that I enjoy administration much anyway.[1] I am called to preach, and love to reach the unreached. God has graciously allowed me to see about one thousand souls at the altar seeking since the General Assembly. This is the joy of my life.

"I don't care to sit in the chair and say, 'You have heard the report. What are we to do with it?' I want to lead the poor lost to Christ. I want to go up among those Indians Brother and Sister Hodgin tell us so much about. Mrs. Rees, as well as myself, is boiling over with Mexico.

"I am pressed on every hand, it seems, to the limit. I did not retire last night until after midnight. I have no hard-luck story; I am going on and up, and the sooner I go up the better. Keep a stiff upper lip. Smile through your tears. Stretch a rainbow across the blackest cloud that ever threatens your sky. The battle will soon be over, and you will march an army of those Indians across the rolling plains of heaven.

With tender Christian love,

Your brother,

SETH C. REES."

But Seth Rees's parish overflowed in more than one missionary direction. It had as high as twenty-one for-

[1] Written after he became General Superintendent of the Pilgrim Holiness Church.

LOG HOUSE, WESTFIELD, INDIANA
WHERE SETH COOK REES WAS BORN

SETH REES WITH MRS. REES
AND REV. R. WINGROVE IVES
AT GEORGETOWN, BRITISH GUIANA, 1932

SETH REES
WITH BISHOP JUJI NAKADA
TOKYO, JAPAN, 1925

SETH COOK REES
AS HE APPEARED IN 1900

eign missionaries on its roll, including such distinguished workers as Mrs. Charles Cowman and Rev. and Mrs. E. L. Kilbourne of the Oriental Missionary Society, and Miss Jennie V. Hughes and Dr. Mary Stone, of the Bethel Mission, Shanghai.

During the years from 1920 to 1925, when Pilgrim Tabernacle was so effectively projecting its full-salvation testimony abroad, its ageing pastor was laboring arduously for the maintenance of its spiritual glow and the extension of its community influence. His Sunday morning sermons, as regards their preparation, were soaked in prayers and tears. Sunday nights were intensely evangelistic, rarely a service passing without an invitation and a response. The mid-week service, promptly begun and early closed, was conducted with a firm hand which had, nevertheless, an extremely sensitive spiritual touch. The calls he made in the homes of his parish were a benediction even when they were brief, as they usually were. Spiritual interests were paramount. His prayer was the high point of his visit. The last year that he served as a pastor, at the age of three score and ten, with manifold responsibilities other than those immediately imposed by his relation to the church, he made nearly four hundred calls. His was a shepherd heart; he devotedly loved and served his flock.

CHAPTER X

CRUSADING ABROAD

WHEN "the great 'Navajo' train of the famous Santa Fe System rolled out of Pasadena at 9:30 a. m., on March 16," 1925, it carried Seth Rees and his wife, their daughter, Evangeline, and their youngest son, Seth Jr. It was the beginning of a world tour of evangelism. In New York City, on the eve of sailing, they were joined by the author. The ten months that followed, packed with activity and overflowing with variety, represented unquestionably a high point in Seth Rees's career. Through the few years that remained to him he looked back upon this experience with undisguised joy and satisfaction, his only regret being that he was unable to spend more time on certain fields where his ministry was particularly fruitful.

Four months were spent in England and Scotland where he found many open doors and left many warm friends. Delightful days were passed in Sweden, his wife's birthplace. Belgium, France and Italy were crossed *en route* to the Mediterranean, Egypt and Palestine. Three weeks in the Holy Land became one of memory's garden spots. Then came the long sail to the Orient and wonderful weeks of spiritual harvesting in China and Japan.

An account of these months of travel was given first

in the form of weekly letters written for the *Pilgrim Holiness Advocate* and, later, in the form of a book entitled WINGS OF THE MORNING. The characteristically "Reesian" letters, which *Advocate* readers had enjoyed, were edited and compiled by the present writer, and sent out for the pleasure and profit of a larger public. In keeping with the purpose to make Part I of this memoir as autobiographical as possible, some selections from WINGS OF THE MORNING are here reproduced. His comments and descriptions are highly varied. Always simple and realistic, they nevertheless ran the whole gamut of emotions from the tragic and pathetic, through the humorous, up the sublime and the superbly spiritual.

Speaking of the voyage to England, he says:

"The purser came to our room to engage us to preach at 10:30 Sunday morning. First, he must assure us that there were no straps on us for the service. This done, we were glad tc take the opportunity to preach on the largest ship afloat. For once we made the godless musicians play and sing, 'Jesus, Lover of My Soul,' 'How Sweet the Name of Jesus Sounds,' and 'My Faith Looks Up to Thee.' The service seemed a little dry—not much like a holiness camp meeting—but the purser was very much broken up, and gripped our hand, thanking us most heartily. At the close of the service an old saint came up and said, 'I heard you preach in Boston long years ago.' I concluded I had better walk straight, as I am not able to get away from my shadow and they have tracked me out to sea."

Recording his impression of a visit to St. Paul's Cathedral, in London, he observes:

"The funeral car of the Duke of Wellington is the wonder of the crypt. It is made entirely from the melted cannons which he captured from Napoleon at Waterloo. It was used to bear the body of the great conqueror to its last resting place. The car weighs nineteen tons, and was built in eighteen days. At his funeral it was drawn by twelve black horses. How fitting that the spoils of that gigantic struggle of his life should bear him to his final resting place!

"Is it possible that the spoils taken in the spiritual conquests of Christian life may be beaten into our triumphal car to bear us to our final Home on High? It is certain that the souls we have captured from the enemy will march with us in the great Royal Review in the 'ages to come.'"

While in London he sought out the hidden-away Quaker burying ground in which rests the honored dust of George Fox. Of this experience he says:

"With the remains of George Fox we tarried in deep meditation. We have just read again the tragic story of his many imprisonments. He was so aggressive, so daring and so fearless that rather than compromise a hair's breadth he would defy the British throne. They could take his head off, but he would not take his hat off. We felt honored to be allowed to drop a flower on the grave of such a hero."

Standing on the tombstone of John Wesley's father, which the illustrious son was once forced to take for his pulpit, Seth Rees's heart was stirred, as will be seen from the following:

"Epworth is a quaint old town of only a few thousand people, nestling among the hills of one of the most charming, picturesque portions of England. It is the birth-place of Methodism, the greatest evangelical movement since the first century. We visited the parish house where John Wesley was born, and saw the window from which he was rescued at the age of six when the house was partially destroyed by fire.

"It was here that his father, Samuel Wesley, was rector for thirty-nine years, during which time John often preached in his father's pulpit. But his father's successor had him ejected from the chapel, whereupon he climbed up on his father's tombstone in the old church yard and preached to the eager throng. We felt a new inspiration as we stood on that same stone and remembered that eventful occasion. It was when the man was put out of the synagogue that Jesus took him in. It may have been Wesley's ejection that gave birth to the movement which swept millions into the kingdom during the first century of its existence."

Edinburgh held for Seth Rees no interest keener than its monuments and memories associated with the name of Scotland's rugged reformer, John Knox. He wept as he stood on the threshold of the little room where Knox was wont to pray. He recalled that Queen Mary said of this "heaven-stormer" that she feared his prayers more than she feared an army.

"As a galley slave (he wrote) Knox wore a shirt of the coarsest canvas, a jacket of serge cut in such a way that he could use his arms freely in rowing, his hair cropped close, and a little cap on his head. From four to six slaves were chained to one bench, on which they sat and rowed through the day and under which they slept at night in all kinds of weather, yet his expression to James Balfour showed that he never lost courage. When, one day, the galley came in sight of the Church of St. Andrews, and Knox caught sight of its steeples, he said to Balfour, his companion at the oar, 'There is the church where I first preached, and where I am certain I will one day preach again.'

"It is no wonder that Regent Morton stood by Knox's grave and said, 'Here lies one who neither flattered nor feared any flesh.' God give us a similar courage in fighting the battles of true holiness against sin and worldliness."

He moralizes on the Battle of Waterloo:

"Yesterday we took a tram car and went to Waterloo. Here sixty thousand men fell in five hours and a half. That fatal October Sunday witnessed one of the most tragic charges of all time. Here Napoleon made the mistake of his life, and went from the highest pinnacle of fame to exile and dishonor on a lonely island.

"His was the mistake that millions are making today. He simply failed to reckon on what is known as the 'Sunken Road,' which was a sudden drop from the level of the battle field into a marsh on the Victor Hugo farm. When Napoleon's cavalry and artillery went over the embankment, escape was impossible. The 'Sunken Road' was filled with dead Frenchmen, over whom Wellington and Blucher marched their armies to victory. Teeming millions are this hour rushing on pellmell to a 'Sunken Road,' an awful declivity, and into the marshes of eternal night from which there is no escape.

"As we stood on these bloody fields we remembered that the Duke of Wellington said, 'This was the hardest battle I have ever fought, and the greatest victory I have ever won.' Remember, Christian soldier, that your greatest conflicts may become your greatest achievements. Let us wring from our foes the strength they seek to take from us, and convert our trials into triumphs."

Those who knew Seth Rees can easily understand the appeal that Savonarola's Florence (Italy) made to him.

"When passing through the room (he says) where Savonarola spent the last night before he was burned at the stake, we allowed the party to go on. We felt that we wanted to be alone for a few moments in that sacred room. We knelt in prayer and were greatly blessed. We said, 'If Savonarola spent his last night on earth in this room, angel feet have pressed this floor and celestial light adorned these walls.' When we stood on the spot in the open square where he and two of his sympathizers were burned, we were reminded that when the Pope wrote him that he was going to excommunicate him from the church, he wrote back: 'From the Church militant you may excommunicate me, but from the Church triumphant never!' When we sat in the church where he denounced the sins of the papacy and thundered forth the gospel of Jesus Christ, we undergirded all our resolutions and strengthened all our purposes to be loyal to Christ and never compromise a hair's breadth."

At three score years and ten Seth Rees entered the ancient city of Jerusalem.

"To get to Jerusalem (he says) we had to ascend twenty-five hundred feet. The mountains are rugged, the canyons deep, the curves sharp and the grades stiff. When the train officials called out 'Jerusalem,' the emotional thrill was indescribable. You may do as I have done—read about it for fifty years—but you will never get the thrill from books however well written, or lectures however well delivered. O Jerusalem, Jerusalem, with deepest emotion we greet thee! 'Our feet shall stand within thy gates, O Jerusalem.' 'As the mountains are round about Jerusalem, so the Lord is round about his people from henceforth even forever.' "

The æsthetic, the imaginative and the descriptive are packed into one of the few "purple patches" that appear in his travel letters:

"The sunsets on the Red Sea and Indian Ocean are gorgeous to the limit. The tropical sky has a deeper, richer blue, and the southern waters have a greater variety of tints than can be found anywhere else. Sometimes the sun looks like a great world on fire, slowly settling down into the sea, appearing first as a fractional eclipse, then half, then three quarters, and finally only a rim of fire—and all is over. One naturally thinks, what if it should never return?

"At other times there is present a great variety of clouds, all shapes and sizes, each contributing a peculiar tint, each reflecting a beauty indescribable. The pearly grey and delicate pink of sky and sea charm us for but a moment, for the grey and pink quickly give way to orange, and this in turn to a fiery red as the sun blazes his silent beauty across the dome of heaven, and the great Indian Ocean seems to stretch away into a southern eternity. As soon as the sun is gone, the star-light begins to be reflected on the restless waters as we whip them into foam. And then, as the after-glow of the setting sun mirrors itself on the broad, smooth surface of the great sea around us, I look, and a full moon hangs low in the eastern sky. And I say, 'It is no use trying'; I can never describe this tropical beauty, by day or by night."

Here are flashes from his account of the great revival work in China and Japan:

"Not less than three hundred seekers were at the altar during the first three days (Shanghai).

"Ninety seekers at the altar yesterday and more than fifty tonight. To God be all the glory!

"Do not tell me that the heathen do not break up and weep.

"Counting the number of seekers at the altar in each service, we saw more than a thousand in the twelve days (Shanghai). I do not know how many came twice or three times, but many came through the first time they came. It was a gracious revival and much of it will live forever."

That these words were a true statement and an accurate prophecy, the succeeding years have clearly shown. To single out only one case, it may be recorded that Andrew Ghi, who was baptized with the Holy Ghost and fire in the Shanghai meetings, has become a mighty soul-winner. He stands today as one of China's most successful evangelists. He says:

"I am very sad to hear of the home-going of your dear father, who labored for the good of the people and the glory of the Lord, for some scores of years all over the world. It is a great loss to the churches and a gain to him, for 'Blessed are the dead which die in the Lord from henceforth: Yea, saith the Spirit, that they may rest from their labors; and their works do follow them.'

"It is a blessed memory in my life that the Lord sent His old faithful servant to China in the winter of 1925. I remember the first night he had a meeting in the Methodist Church, in Shanghai, and preached on the text of Acts 1:8. He did not preach long, but he gave the invitation, for which I am still praising the Lord. The Holy Spirit moved my heart. I went forward, praying for the blessed Holy Ghost to fall upon my soul. I received Him by faith. Since that night the Lord has worked in me and through. Praise the Lord for that day!"

A soul-winner from the day he received his Pentecost, Andrew Ghi has been particularly blessed of God in the ministry of the past three years. He is the chief speaker in the Bethel Evangelistic Band, organized in 1931. In two years and a half the Band has ministered in seventeen provinces of China, their efforts meeting with extraordinary success. More than 35,000 conversions and sanctifications have been witnessed.

Seth Rees was profoundly impressed and greatly cheered by the excellent missionary work that he saw was being done by the Oriental Missionary Society, under the leadership of the now sainted Rev. E. A. Kilbourne, and by the Bethel Mission, under the direction of Dr. Mary Stone and Miss Jennie V. Hughes.

Of a convention in Tokyo, Japan, where he was the guest of Bishop Juji Nakada, he says:

"Five lepers came from the leper colony away up in the mountains, where six hundred lepers are congregated, many of whom are saved and sanctified wholly. They said they were sent for two purposes: to express the colony's appreciation of the fact that we intended to visit them (we would have done so but for sickness) and to get some "crumbs" to carry back to their fellows in affliction. Their salutation was most touching. They kept their hands in their pockets and were careful to come in contact with no one.

"It was most interesting to see eight hundred or a thousand people sitting on the floor, so eager to hear the gospel that no one moves no difference how long the message. We never think of urging people to come to the altar; we rather insist that they shall not come unless they are definite seekers for pardon or purity, and yet they come by the scores and by the hundreds. Out of a congregation of a thousand people we have seen two hundred and fifty on their knees and on their faces seeking the Lord."

The long journey was not without its grey days. In England, in Palestine and in Japan sickness laid a heavy hand on members of the family. In Kobe, Japan, Seth Junior nearly succumbed to a vicious case of smallpox. Always a tender sympathizer with his wife and children in their distresses, the husband and father bore these afflictions as if they had been his own. Once or twice, indeed, they were his own. Pathos and humor mingle in the following:

"We have been recording many of the beautiful, charming and wonderful things of travel, and have purposely left unrecorded all that was inconvenient, trying or disappointing. But why should we 'receive good at the hand of the Lord, and not evil?' Why should we not record, and rejoice over, our trials as well as our triumphs?

"Soon after arriving in England three of the family were taken down with the 'flu.' And, after kind friends have done all they can do, 'flu is flu,' with all its consequences. I doubt if Satan ever spoke to me more definitely than he did at this time. I was one of the three victims, flat on my back, and he regarded this as his chance. He first said, 'You are a fool.' Well, that was not so far off; but he proceeded to tell me why. 'You are a fool to take your family abroad when you knew that the "flu" was raging in England. You will bury a part of your family in Europe among strangers.' I saw the coffins and the graves. I said, 'It doesn't matter about me, for unless the Lord comes I will be buried in a few years, somewhere.' But when he threatened the younger members of the family, I confess the sweat broke out on my body. They were then in great pain.

"Mrs. Rees certainly had her hands full, nursing the three of us. It became necessary for us to change quarters. Though we were paying a good price for board, with third-story sleeping rooms, we found that the beds were inhabited and the occupants were miserable comforters. It was providentially and circumstantially dark.

"I called to mind a lot of my own preaching, times when I had swung across the platform and gesticulated furiously, preaching from the text, 'Where sin abounded, grace did much more abound,' or the text, 'And the iron did swim.' 'Well,' I said, 'the preaching was all right; and though it doesn't seem that the iron is swimming, things are not as they seem to be.' Then I would announce to the powers of darkness: 'The iron does swim!' and quote texts to support it. 'All things work together for good!' 'All things are possible to him that believeth!' 'He shall abide with you forever!'

"Then I was reminded how I had pranced about in the pulpit, and told the saints how they could 'smile through their tears, and span the darkest cloud with a rainbow.' Then I yanked myself up and said, 'Are you doing that? Here is a chance to practice your own preaching.' I said, 'Yes, I may not look like it, but I am,' and away down in my soul I laughed aloud. I faced the regiments of hell, and declared that though 'weeping may endure for a night, joy cometh in the morning.' I rose up in the strength of Jehovah. With joy I record that there never was a moment when I did not want the will of God more than anything else; and I did not hesitate to tell Satan that I would rather be in hell with Jesus than to be in heaven with him. It was real, and the triumph was correspondingly great, for we went out from the storm cloud to see hundreds of souls weep their way to the Cross."

With his arrival at Pasadena, in January, 1926, Seth Rees joyfully and gratefully completed his world tour.

CHAPTER XI

THE GENERAL

WE have come to the closing period in the active life of the Warrior-Saint. It covers exactly six years, from the autumn of 1926, when he was elected a General Superintendent of the Pilgrim Holiness Church, to the autumn of 1932, when a severe illness forced his retirement to the little bungalow, in Pasadena, where he was confined almost continuously until the time of his passing.

In the summer of 1926 death, for the third time, invaded the circle of children to whom Seth Rees had rejoiced to be a father. It had taken Loring, his second son by Hulda Rees, in 1913, and Byron, his eldest, in 1919. This time it claimed his youngest, Seth Cook Junior, a lad of seventeen who was a most promising musician and a devoted Christian. "I am convulsed with sorrow" is a line from the bereaved father's journal, expressive of the grief he bore through the months that followed this great loss. Yet so firm was his faith in the Unerring Goodness that no murmur marred the sweetness or serenity of his communion with the Holy Spirit; instead, a new note of tenderness and sympathy sounded like some rich undertone in his ministry.

In September the General Assembly of the Pilgrim Holiness Church convened at Frankfort, Indiana. It insistently turned to Seth Rees for leadership. The new responsibility was accepted with only partial knowledge of the tax that would be levied on declining physical energies. For four years the Superintendency was shared by two other brethren, one whose duty it was to direct the foreign mission activities of the church, another to divide the care of affairs in the United States. Then the load became heavier. During his last two years of service the entire general oversight of the denomination, at home and abroad, was organized under one Superintendency. Notwithstanding the assistance given by efficient lieutenants, it was a stressful burden for any man to carry, especially so for one who had passed his seventy-fifth milestone. The church numbered 17,000 members, nearly 500 local societies, more than 600 ordained ministers, and close to 450 missionaries and native workers.

Along with the responsibilities normally belonging to his office, such as presiding over assemblies and board meetings, and conducting a necessarily heavy correspondence, there were two types of service Seth Rees continued to render with unabated zeal. He persistently pressed revivalism in his preaching and he quite as persistently promoted the cause of publications, particularly the *Pilgrim Holiness Advocate.* To this paper he was a regular contributor during the last ten years of his life.

One of the most powerful and resultful revivals of his last years occurred in Asheville, N. C., early in the fall of 1927. Mr. J. L. Crouse and his son, Byron, fire-baptized laymen from Greensboro, pitched a large tent, provided a band of capable musicians, and announced Seth Rees as their evangelist. The meeting ran for three weeks, the last two of which witnessed a tidal wave of true Pentecostal evangelism. Great crowds filled the tent, great anointing rested upon the preacher. Between four and five hundred knelt at the altar as definite seekers. An exceptionally high proportion of them went away with a testimony. The preacher's heart was overflowing with gladness, as the following diary excerpts show:

August 30—"Sixty-three seekers at the altar. Have seen nothing like it since I left Japan. How bold the converts! Came on the platform and witnessed. He gets all the glory!"

September 5—"Preached at 8, on the Second Coming again. Twenty-eight seekers. Wonderful meeting! Wonderful cases! Retired at 12 but could not sleep. All glory to God!"

September 9—"Preached at night. Thirty-four at the altar. Thirty got through. One of the most wonderful meetings I have ever witnessed."

Not in many years had Seth Rees contended with such generally poor health as he did in 1928. The first two months were spent in tent campaigning in Florida. In these meetings he and the author—father and son—were delightfully associated. In March, however, he returned to Pasadena where much of the year was passed in a condition of depleted strength and curtailed activities. Yet he was far from idle. Supplying an interim vacancy in the pastorate of the Pilgrim Tabernacle, he preached regularly in his old pulpit for a period of several months.

Early in the spring of 1929, his health apparently much improved, he resumed the rounds of administrative and evangelistic responsibilities. After conducting a revival and an annual assembly in Owosso, Mich., he proceeded to Gloversville, N. Y., for a similar engagement. Here he was taken gravely ill. It was a heart attack. In ordering him home the attending physician advised him to take a long rest, picturesquely reminding him that his condition might be likened to that of a "Ford motor in a Packard car." The rest, at Pasadena, proved not to be a long one. Feeling that God had touched his body into new strength and fitness, the warrior soon returned to the battle. Before the summer was over his ripened ministries had been conferred for good upon widely different sections of the nation—Colorado, Ohio, Kentucky, and West Virginia.

He was ever the prophet; the unexpected might be expected when he was in action. A business session might become a Pentecost. Just before leaving California for these eastern appointments he was invited to deliver the Commencement Sermon at the Huntington Park Training School for Christian Workers, Los Angeles. The address was so charged with spiritual dynamics, with a fervor that was at once evangelical and evangelistic, that several persons made their way to the altar eager for the experience of "power from on high"; and the whole occasion was so unique and Pentecostal that it elicited from the now sainted Dr. G. A. McLaughlin, who was then on the faculty of the institution, a highly appreciative editorial in *The Christian Witness*.

For miles traveled, engagements filled, sermons preached, burdens carried and—most important of all to the preacher—souls won to the dear Redeemer, 1930 proved to be an extraordinary year. As might be imagined, it witnessed a marked return of his accustomed physical vigor. Some of his friends remarked that he looked ten years younger than he did the year preceding. Before the twelve months expired he had traveled approximately fifteen thousand miles, crossing the continent from ocean to ocean not less than four times. Included in his itinerary in this seventy-sixth year of his life were annual assemblies, conventions and evangelistic campaigns in Denton, Md., Lansing and Flint, Mich., Albany and Brooklyn, N. Y., Upland and Frankfort, Ind., Newkirk, Okla., Portsmouth, R. I., Huntington, W. Va., Allentown, Pa., Portsmouth and Troy, Ohio, and Pasadena, Calif.

Of his work in the District Assembly at Denton the reporter wrote:

"Our General Superintendent, Seth C. Rees, with his esteemed wife, won all our hearts. It is doubtful if this great preacher ever did greater preaching than he did in Denton. His sermons were indeed in the power and demonstration of the Spirit."

"I shall never cease to thank God that we were able to have him in one of our Annual Brooklyn Holiness Conventions," wrote Mrs. C. H. Cooke, recalling his ministry to that gathering in November, 1930. "It seems to me that no preacher has been more signally honored of God. I do not think that anyone will ever forget his messages in that convention. The people of my Tuesday afternoon meeting still talk of them. . . . The tenderness of his wonderful face, the gentle cadence of his voice, will be among the most precious memories of Brother Cooke and myself, even until the day break and the shadows flee away."

The first nine months of 1931 witnessed no abatement in the intensity of activity which had characterized the preceding year. From January to April the General Superintendent's time was occupied largely with conducting brief conventions in Ohio, Pennsylvania, Delaware, Maryland and New Jersey. Besides aiming directly at conversions and sanctifications, these gatherings subserved the purpose of firing the interest of the churches in home and foreign missions. How his ministry was impressing others may be gathered from a report of the convention held in Allentown, Pa. The account was furnished by a minister and reads in part:

"It was my inestimable privilege to hear the Rev. Seth C. Rees, General Superintendent of the Pilgrim Holiness Church, preach the unadulterated Gospel of Jesus Christ in its pristine purity and power as it is seldom heard anywhere nowadays. This anointed, holy messenger of God did not mince matters as he from night to night fearlessly, yet in tenderness and love, unfolded to his hearers the stern truths of the Bible. Brother Rees's style is simple and unaffected, rising at times to genuine flights of oratory. . . . True to Bible doctrines, an able expositor of New Testament Christianity, a hater of hypocrisy and shams, a lover of immortal souls and an exceptionally clear thinker, he may well be styled 'Prince of Evangelists.' "

Seth Rees's own account of the convention held at Dover, Del., contains, incidentally, some comments so characteristic that his friends will read them here with a smile of instant recognition.

"On the closing day (he writes) more than thirty seekers were at the altar and nearly all tunneled through in old-time manner. One whole family was converted, sinners repenting and shouting the victory; to see sixteen come through bright, at one clip, is a sight for angels to behold and cause devils to turn pale. I love Brother .... (the pastor), but that is not all; I *like* him. . . . I like his spirit. I like his brief announcements. He does not repeat and then exhort until it is too late to preach. I like his easy quiet way of taking an offering. . . . I like him because he gets me to preaching before the congregation goes to sleep. One preacher exhorted so much with his announcements that strangers thought that was the sermon and got up and went home. Brother C.... did not speel and spill until it was too late to preach. Brother, take the hint; 'go and do thou likewise.'"

Having completed the convention itinerary, Seth Rees conducted a fruitful revival in the Tabernacle of the Detroit Holiness Association, Detroit, Mich., presided over district assemblies in Binghamton, N. Y., and Battle Creek, Mich., rested a bit at Long Beach, Calif., and then plunged into camp meeting labors. But it proved to be a summer of much pain and handicap. Two of his engagements were cut short by illness. After a brief respite, however, he was back "at the front." In August he was able to minister to the thousands that came to the great camp at Wichita, Kansas. It was a privilege he welcomed for reasons suggested by the following excerpts from his account of the meeting:

"After a run of a thousand miles I found myself at Wichita, Kansas. This is the greatest camp west of Chicago, and not only great but glorious. These devout westerners were not picnicking. They came to get help and to help others. . . . Those who kept count said that there were about five hundred seekers at the mourner's bench. It was reported that there were eight thousand people on the ground the first Sunday. God enabled me to take my turn and preach once every day of the camp. . . .

"It is thirty-two years since the writer attended this camp, at which time Mrs. Mitchel shouted herself through the Golden Gates and her remains lay on the greensward while the writer preached and the long altar filled with seekers. . . . The camp is forty-two years old. When we were asked to conduct a Hallelujah March in making a free-will offering for camp expenses, a spry lady, 95 years old, who had never been absent from the camp in all these years, led the march. It was thrilling. Many states were represented in that great march."

A parenthesis of nine weeks drops into the closing quarter of 1931. During these weeks Seth Rees was confined in the Deaconess Hospital at Marshalltown, Iowa, undergoing operations for cataracts on his eyes. Emerging from this trying experience with slowly improving sight, he and Mrs. Rees set forth, early in January, for the West Indies and South America. Mrs. Rees accompanied him, as she did almost incessantly in the travels of his last few years.

"Mrs. Rees and I felt clearly (he writes) that we should visit South America and the islands of the Caribbean Sea. For several years we had been saving up a little money for such a trip, and early in 1932 we sailed out of New York harbor on the beautiful 'Monarch of Bermuda.' The ship on which we booked passage carried much freight and it happened that they accepted a shipment of gasoline, which made it unlawful for them to carry passengers; so the only thing they could do was to transfer us to the splendid 'Monarch,' giving us first class passage with only second class charges.

"It was a charming trip to Bermuda. Mrs. Rees and I rested and praised the Lord for His goodness to us all along the way. Our ship was such a fast one she got into Bermuda harbor two days ahead of the time we were supposed to get in on the semi-freight boat. They put us in a fine hotel on Saturday and we remained there until Monday without additional expense. This afforded an opportunity to see the Island of Bermuda. One must do his sight-seeing by horse and buggy. No motor cars are allowed on the island. All the Bermudas are beautiful resorts.

"By Monday morning our ship, the 'Maraval,' had arrived and unloaded her gasoline. So we went aboard. She traveled so slowly and the sea was so rough that we had about four hundred hours of nerve strain. The roll and pitch were terrifically trying."

Touching at St. Martins and sighting successively Saba, St. Kitts, St. Vincent and Grenada, then touching at Port of Spain, Trinidad, they landed for their first engagement at Georgetown in British Guiana.

"We received a most cordial and kind welcome (writes Seth Rees) from many missionaries and laymen. The Pilgrim Church has little conception of the culture and eloquence we have in these southern missionaries and native workers. When we were all assembled in an auditorium for the welcome service, those black folk showed such respect for the servants of the Lord that I had to bow my head on my Bible and weep. One of the native preachers, as black as night, delivered the address of welcome. It was extemporaneous but eloquent to the limit, and delivered in such a musical tone that I hated to see the fellow sit down. After such a masterful and musical address I was at a loss to know how to answer him. I made a staggering attempt and failed, yet in my heart I meant all that I was trying to say to them.

"Our few days at Georgetown were full of blessing. Some of the leaders said it was the greatest meeting ever held in the city. There were those of the *élite* of the city who were reached, and many who had never been in our church before were present and gave most careful attention to the preaching of the gospel. A great number of souls were thus reached and saved. There were more than three hundred seekers at the penitent form, among them many new cases.

"Before leaving Georgetown we embraced the opportunity to visit the grave of Brother C. O. Moulton, who was really the pioneer missionary of our work in the West Indies and South America. We little knew what we were doing when at Portsmouth Camp Meeting, Rhode Island, we raised the money and sent him to these islands more than twenty years ago. He not only reaped a great harvest of souls during his brief life but fruit remains and abounds to this day. After a brief prayer and a tear at this sacred spot, we turned to the wharf to board our ship for Trinidad where our next convention was held.

"Trinidad is the largest of the lesser Antilles. It is rather a bit of the South American continent and only separated from the mainland by the narrow Bocas. The capital, Port of Spain, has a population of about 70,000. Nearly one third of the number are East Indians, while those of African descent are in the majority. Mohammedan mosques, Hindu temples and Confucian meeting-places are much in evidence. The island is one of nature's beauty spots.

"It seemed that the date of our convention in Trinidad was unpropitious, as this was the week immediately preceding the great annual Catholic carnival. When we saw the situation we threw ourselves recklessly on the Holy Ghost and cried persistently for His intervention. He answered promptly and we had one hundred seekers at the penitent form on the first day of the assembly. Our attendance was much smaller than it would have been at other times, but the power of God was the same and He wrought mightily in saving sinners, reclaiming backsliders and sanctifying believers. Rev. and Mrs. O. W. Rees have labored effectively on this island for ten years.

"From Trinidad we sailed to Barbados, the most easterly of the West Indian Islands. Bridgetown is the capital; it has a population of about 17,000. The island, twenty-one miles long and fourteen wide, has a population of nearly 170,000. On our arrival in Bridgetown we were most cordially greeted by a large number of Pilgrims, and were at once conducted to the residence of Rev. and Mrs. R. W. Ives, where we were made to feel much at home."

Seth Rees's modesty precluded reference to the personal discomforts and handicaps with which he had to contend in these island travels. R. W. Ives, traveling with him and marvelling at his courage and faith, was moved to write:

"One of the outstanding characteristics of Brother Rees was a remarkable power of will that kept him at the battle's front when otherwise he might have been laid aside. A case or two in point. On the voyage to British Guiana, during a storm, he was thrown with terrific force against some iron rails and evidently fractured some of his ribs. Not to disconcert Mrs. Rees, he refrained from relating the actual facts. On his arrival in Georgetown he was in a bad condition, but he went into the great convention in the Pilgrim Tabernacle as if nothing unusual had happened. The journeys back and forth to the meetings from the Mission House were extremely painful, and with every jar of the car he suffered greatly, but personal discomfort never caused him to slow down, notwithstanding the added unpleasantness of the trying Guianese climate.

"Again, as we were leaving Trinidad Brother Rees became quite ill. We entertained some fear as to the advisability of going on to Barbados by the boat we had planned to take. Once more his indomitable will subdued his feelings and urged him on in the campaign for souls. When we reached Barbados, his condition was so serious that he called in a doctor who ordered him to cancel all preaching arrangements and rest until he was sufficiently recovered to return to the United States. This was Saturday night. The great opening of the Barbados Convention was planned, and announced throughout the churches on the island, for Sunday morning. As Superintendent I hardly knew what to do at that late hour, for we anticipated a tremendous attendance at the Whitepark Pilgrim Tabernacle, where the meetings were to be held. We realized that the disappointment of the West Indian saints would be very keenly felt if the General Superintendent were not able to be present.

"After the doctor and Mrs. Rees had left the room, Brother Rees turned to me and said, 'Brother Ives, God didn't send me to the Caribbean to lie around sick, but to preach the gospel, and I am going to church in the morning.' We then had a season of prayer and committed the case to the Lord.

"The next morning I went to church early. We received fifty-two into the society. We carried out the preliminaries. The church was crowded to its uttermost capacity with a congregation estimated at between eight hundred and a thousand. That grand old hymn, 'The Comforter Has Come,' was being sung with soul-inspiring feeling. Just as the strains of the third stanza were struck up—

'Lo, the great King of kings, with healing in His wings,
To ev'ry captive soul a full deliv'rance brings;
An thro' the vacant cells the song of triumph rings;
The Comforter has come!'—

Brother and Sister Rees entered the door leading onto the rostrum. Never have we felt the presence of the Holy Ghost in a service as we did on that occasion. The sight of that great concourse of Pilgrims, together with our beloved General Superintendent, waving their handkerchiefs, their upturned faces bespeaking their unspeakable joy, made one feel that Pentecost was a glorious reality even in these last and awful days.

"Then Brother Rees preached with unusual unction, and eighty souls responded to the appeal. In the week's meeting that followed God gave Brother Rees 513 souls at the altar. The memory of those days will live in the years to come; it will recall one of the greatest meetings held in the Pilgrim Church in Barbados."

Physical disability prevented the completion of the Caribbean itinerary. The voyage home was a rough one, which added nothing to Seth Rees's convalescence. Landing at Boston in the early spring, he and Mrs. Rees proceeded to the home of friends in Maryland for a much needed rest. Later in the spring and throughout the summer he preached with considerable vigor, and drove through to the discharge of his official duties with unremitting toil and persistency.

It was a beautiful morning late in August, 1932. Seth Rees, visiting the Mount of Praise Camp Meeting, Circleville, Ohio, where the author was ministering as evangelist, was presented to an eager audience to deliver a missionary address. He stepped to the front of the platform, his large Bible open in his left hand, and read his text: "How beautiful upon the mountains are the feet of him that bringeth good tidings, that publisheth peace." (ISAIAH 52:7). For thirty minutes his flaming soul was like a torch to light and kindle the souls of his brothers and sisters in Christ. It was a high hour. Little did the son, who now writes these lines in grateful remembrance, realize that he was listening to the last public address he would ever hear from his father's lips.

Days of pain and privation from service were just ahead. It was the beginning of the end!

CHAPTER XII

THE DISCHARGE HONORABLE

"THERE is," observed Samuel A. Tipple, "one chapter in the biography of distinguished persons—in the biography of a great genius, an eminent saint or seer—which has for us generally special interest, into which we are often most curious to dip—the chapter entitled 'Closing Days,' curious to learn how he bore himself, or what fell from his lips during those days in the shadow of the approaching end, to see something of the thoughts that then expressed his mind, or to hear something of his latest words. What of his behaviour, his expression, we ask, in his latest hours? The favourite pursuit—was its influence upon him then exemplified? The ruling passion—was it strong with him in death?"

The last eight months of Seth Rees's life were spent in forced retirement, much of the time in weakness and pain. In September, 1932, he was helped from the train at Pasadena, a sick and, as subsequent events proved, a broken man. Rallying a bit before the month was over, he undertook to conduct a series of meetings a few miles from home. He was unable to finish. His last sermon was preached from LUKE 16:23—"In hell he lift up his eyes, being in torments, and seeth Abraham afar off, and Lazarus in his bosom." It was a message of contrasts—life and death, heaven and hell, wooing and warning. It was a small meeting but there were several who presented themselves at the altar to "flee from the wrath to come" and "lay hold upon eternal life." To the end his cry was "Souls!" And to the end God heard that cry. The next day he was so ill his engagement had to be cancelled.

His case was not correctly diagnosed until many weeks of valuable time had been lost. Although there were days when he was unable to leave his room, his indomitable will and his God-centered hope kept him on his feet and held him to the attempted discharge of his official duties when he should have been in bed, completely relaxed and resting. When finally a true diagnosis was reached, it was too late. An extremely overworked heart would not respond to the quiet and care that were prescribed.

As spring followed winter the decline continued. Days of relief from pain were succeeded by nights of suffering. Intervals of quickened strength were followed by lapses into almost unbearable weakness.

Through it all there was a quenchless zeal for the cause of Christ: for the prosperity of Zion and for the salvation of men everywhere. The "ruling passion" ruled to the end. Tenderly, painstakingly he would trace in prayer the course of missions through the nations. As his fervent intercessions ascended, now from his bed and now from his wheel-chair, many missionaries were mentioned by name. He dictated letters to them, urging them on in the "good fight." They needed funds; he had some offering to send. They faced problems; he had some suggestion to offer. They were in distress; he had some message of comfort and cheer to dispatch.

As he approached March 17, 1933, he requested that a number of his oldest resident friends and neighbors be invited in for a simple service of celebration. He wished thus to commemorate his conversion on this its sixtieth anniversary. "Very weak," says one who was present, "and sitting propped up in a chair, Brother Rees spoke, slowly and sometimes almost inaudibly but with deep feeling and a smile upon his face, of his conversion and call to preach the Gospel." With considerable detail he recalled the story, given in Chapter I, of his entrance into the Kingdom of God and his setting forth to be an ambassador of the King. After Misses Salome Gross and Lillian Beard had sung one of his favorite hymns, "Amazing Grace," he was saluted by Rev. J. P. Coleman, himself a veteran in the Holy War, with the following original poem:

"How beautiful on this birthday
Assembled in the home,
To know that God has led the way
Along which you have came.

"You've journeyed on and on and on,
O'er moor and plain and glen;
The friends of youth, alas, are gone,
And life has changed since then.

"You've crossed the mountains wild and grand,
Out in the Golden West;
You've found a home in this new land
To spend your days in rest.

"How sweet in these, your closing years,
To dwell with kindred ties,

With life serene and free from fears,
Beneath such balmy skies.

"With wistful gaze we're looking on
Beyond the bounds of time;
Soon we shall all be gathered home,
Where suns forever shine."

One April morning when, having passed a fairly restful night, he had requested that he be wheeled into the parlor, he led in prayer at family worship. He prayed:

"Dear Father, I am uplifted; Thou hast lifted me up. May I continue to be uplifted. I know I am weak, but Thou art my strength.

"Enough for myself! I want to pray for the ends of the earth. The Kingdom! The Kingdom! The Kingdom! I want to fight the powers of darkness. I want to be used of God—to pull down the strongholds of the devil.

"Give me victory! Not my victory; it's Thine.

"God is great. He is greater than ever!

"Hallelujah! Amen!"

Each clause was spoken very deliberately, with profound feeling. The sense of God's encompassing, enfolding presence was ineffably precious.

One day, while dictating, he grew very weak. Pale but smiling, he said, "Sister Neff, I'm living these days with the Glory-World in view. I expect to go in with some of the prisoners of Jesus Christ. Then, when we are all freed from suffering, He will take us to the loftiest mountains and the tallest peaks where we are going to witness the most transcendently glorious scenes in all the roll of the eternities. Oh, I'll praise Him then for all this suffering and pain!"

Yet, like more than one saint facing the "last enemy," Seth Rees had his faith fiercely assaulted. The play of physical and nervous factors in one's spiritual life is not easily understood, but it must be recognized. Taking advantage of these factors, the Prince of Darkness will oppress those whom he cannot possess. But prayer is effectual and faith puts fear to flight, as was demonstrated on two or three occasions in the case of this servant of God. The last steps of the pilgrimage were taken in a strong and steady stride of triumphant faith.

To the Annual Assembly of the Pilgrim Holiness Church of Mexico, which he had hoped to attend, he wrote, in part:

"Dear Beloved:

"I am more than disappointed not to be able to be with you in your Assembly at Valles. I have been sick now almost nine months, but have hoped for the last three months that I would so recover as to be with you and remain some weeks, but I am still in bed with the exception of an hour or two each day.

"I am not overstating when I express to you the deepest sympathy, love, confidence and Christian co-operation in all the work which you are doing. But my heart burns and fairly blazes with a passion for the salvation of the noble tribe of Aztec Indians. Those who have been saved have made such manly men and such successful soul-winners that I wish I could preach the Gospel of Jesus Christ, the Cross and the Blood, to every one of their thousands.

"I feel like flying, but my wings have not been supplied; and I am here under the jurisdiction of one of the most capable and faithful nurses, and missionaries as well, that we have ever had in the Church—Daisy Buby, who has been with us more than six weeks. She, too, has longed to return to Mexico, and again and again we have talked of how we would get to the Assembly.

"With faithful Christian love,
Yours to make Him known,
Seth C. Rees."

In the quotation with which this chapter opened the question is asked concerning the "closing days" of an eminent person, "The favourite pursuit—was its influence upon him then exemplified?" Preaching was Seth Rees's "favourite pursuit," and its influence was upon him to the last. Of this there could be no mistake. One evening he had been wheeled to the center of the parlor. Loved ones were seated around him, including Rev. and Mrs. Arnold Hodgin. Mrs. Hodgin, in a mood of reminiscence, was describing some of the great services of the past in which she had heard him preach. She said she would never forget his sermon from the text, "The secret of the Lord is with them that fear him; and he will show them his covenant." His face lighted up. Raising his right hand in a characteristic gesture, he said, "And this is the way I began—

"The natural world is full of secrets. She is a treasure house of mysteries, of which man knows but little."

Preparing the way, by suggestion and illustration, for the development of his analogy, he continued:

"So there are secrets in the spiritual realm, known only to those who fear the Lord. It is the work of the Holy Ghost to reveal these secrets.

"First, the New Birth is a secret."

And on he went, slowly but feelingly, for a quarter of an hour, until his nurse gently insisted that he must not expend more of his strength. He was reluctant to stop. The fire still burned. Within the old worn bulb flamed a deathless incandescence. With a twinkle in his eye, he said, as he was wheeled from the room, "Come back tomorrow and I'll give you some more."

Not infrequently he experienced the paradox of extreme physical depression and great spiritual exaltation. One day, near the last, in a voice that was a kind of ecstatic whisper, he said to his nurse, "Glory! I'm blessed. I feel the Holy Ghost in my heart. Oh, I feel him all over me. I'm so unworthy of all this love, but He has blessed me beyond words."

When it seemed that he was far too weak for it, he insisted on being wheeled out to the homes of several of his neighbors where he might bear his testimony and offer prayer.

One day, as the consciousness of things present was lessened and that of things to come was heightened, his face lighted up and he exclaimed, "Beautiful! I see Brother Braithwaite (West Indies missionary), Ichinomya (one of his interpreters in Japan),"—and other names were given, but too indistinctly to catch. "We are going to get in; yes, we are going to have an abundant entrance." Much of the time it seemed to him that he was in meetings. "They are coming to get help," he would say, "they are coming by the thousands. They are coming to get the Holy Ghost; they are climbing over each other." The great revival scenes he had witnessed in the Orient and the West Indies were vividly before him, and the names of such fellow workers as Rev. Tetsuji Tsuchiyama, Bishop Juji Nakada, Dr. Mary Stone and Rev. Jennie V. Hughes were often upon his lips.

To his constantly attending wife he said one day, "Don't hold me back, I want to go Home!"

Another day he gently counseled her, "Thee must take up the work which I am laying down. Preach the gospel!"

Sinking steadily as he passed the middle of May, it was impossible for him to move from his bed. His last Sunday on earth was spent in a deep sleep. Just before slipping into this final slumber his lips were seen to move. Into the ears of his preacher-son, who bent over him eagerly, came the whispered words: "I'm—almost —home!"

And so he was. The end came at 3:45 Monday morning, May 22. Just as the day was beginning to break cloudlessly over the mountains of which he was so untiringly fond, he passed from peace to greater peace.

"The storm and the darkness—the desolate night—
But the ship saileth sure, and the harbor's in sight;
And a melody swells
From the chime o' the bells;—
'Home in the beautiful morning.'

"O long was the seaway, with billows to breast;
But we dreamed on those billows of havens of rest;
O'er the ocean's sad knells
Still the chime o' the bells—
'Home in the beautiful morning.'

"O storm and black billows, not hopeless, we roam,
For love guides the ship to the white shores of home;
And the melody swells
From the jubilant bells—
'Home in the beautiful morning.'"

Those lines seemed beautifully appropriate that morning. Since then we have thought several times of Bunyan's incomparable passage descriptive of the crossing of the river and the welcome on the other side. That spiritual genius of Bedford makes Mr. Standfast say:

"I see myself now at the end of my journey; my toilsome days are ended. I am going now to see the head that was crowned with thorns, and that face that was spit upon for me.

"I have formerly lived by hear-say and faith; but now I go where I shall live by sight, and shall be with Him in whose company I delight myself.

"I have loved to hear my Lord spoken of; and wherever I have seen the print of His shoe in the earth, there I have coveted to set my foot, too.

"His name has been to me as a civet-box, yea, sweeter than all perfumes. His voice to me has been most sweet; and His countenance I have more desired than they that have most desired the light of the sun. His Word I did use to gather for my food, and for antidotes against my fainting. He has held me, and I have kept me from mine iniquities: yea, my steps hath He strengthened in His way."

Then follows the gripping story of Standfast's passing:

"Now while he was thus in discourse, his countenance changed; his strong man bowed under him; and after he had said, 'Take me, for I come unto Thee,' he ceased to be seen of them.

"But glorious it was to see how the open region was filled with horses and chariots; with trumpeters and pipers; with singers and players on stringed instruments—to welcome the pilgrims as they went up, and followed one another in at the beautiful gate of the city."

The funeral occurred two days later at Pilgrim Tabernacle. The auditorium was crowded with the hundreds of friends who had come to pay the quiet, in many instances the tearful, tribute of their affection and respect. Impressively they sang one of his favorite hymns, "Jesus Lover of My Soul." Rev. Charles L. Slater offered prayer. Rev. William Neff, who as pastor of the Tabernacle was in charge of the service, read the Scriptures. By this time, as one wrote, "the listeners were rapidly becoming conscious of the fact that this was no ordinary funeral service, not simply because it was being held for a distinguished leader, but particularly because of the presence of the Holy Spirit, the blessed Comforter. It would not have been difficult to convince devoted saints that the very angels of God stood among the flowers and kept vigil at that casket."

After "Amazing Grace" had been rendered instrumentally by Rev. Ross Miner, several brief addresses were made. Rev. Walter L. Surbrook, succeeding to the office of General Superintendent of the Pilgrim Holiness Church, spoke of the loss of leadership which was being so keenly felt throughout the church. Death, he felt, had brought sharply into focus certain traits in the life and ministry of his departed chief, notably his personal piety, his great gifts as a preacher, his loyalty to the Bible and its standards, his uncompromising stand for righteousness. Rev. Paul W. Thomas, General Secretary-Treasurer of the Pilgrim Church, dwelt tenderly on Seth Rees's unceasing, unwaning "interest in the work of the Lord." Here was a man, he felt, whose heart thrilled at the success of evangelism as it did to nothing else in the world. Rev. Lillian Beard, Vice-president of Pilgrim Bible College, drew attention to the many-sidedness of the life of the institution's founder and to the eternal triumph upon which he had honorably entered.

Rev. and Mrs. Edwin Kilbourne, representing the Oriental Missionary Society, sang N. B. Vandall's "My Home, Sweet Home."

"Home, sweet Home; home, sweet Home,
Where I'll never roam,
I see the light of that City so bright—
My Home, sweet Home."

The next tribute was by Rev. J. P. Coleman, senior elder of Pilgrim Tabernacle. Moved with deep emotion, he read a lovely poem which he had composed for the occasion, closing with the lines:

"We'll ne'er behold his like again
Among the sons of men;
His mem'ry and his work remain,
Till all of life shall end."

Rev. I. G. Martin, a long-time friend and neighbor, recalled the battles and triumphs of other days in which he had labored with his esteemed friend, whose ministry he characterized as having been "preeminently inspirational."

The closing address was given by Rev. John S. Kimber, pastor of Trinity Missionary Church, in Los Angeles, one of Seth Rees's beloved friends through a period of forty years. It was a beautiful message, informing in its reminiscences, sincere in its appreciations, charming in its simplicity, comforting in its spirit. He testified that he and Mrs. Kimber received the Baptism with the Holy Spirit at the first session of the camp-meeting founded by Seth Rees at Portsmouth, R. I.

Rev. Joseph Reece, singing "The City Four-Square," lifted before the hushed throng the vision of the "Better Country":

"'God shall wipe away all tears;'
There's no death, no pain, nor fears;
And they count not time by years,
For there is 'no night there.'"

A dying request of Seth Rees's was then observed. For the space of three minutes the congregation joined in "Quaker silence." No spiritually discerning heart failed to sense "The Presence in the Midst." Benediction was pronounced by Rev. William Kirby, and burial followed in Mountain View Cemetery, at Pasadena.

Over the bier, the widow, bowed with grief yet divinely becalmed, intoned the first stanza of "The Christian's Good-night":

> "Sleep on, beloved, sleep, and take thy rest;
> Lay down thy head upon thy Saviour's breast:
> We love well, but Jesus loves thee best—
> Good-night! Good-night!"

CHAPTER XIII

CONCEPTIONS AND CHARACTERISTICS

SINCE Seth Rees lived to preach—more than once his intimates heard him say, "I would rather preach than eat"—we shall begin with his conception of the ministry. "There is," he insisted, "no higher or holier calling on earth or in heaven. It is not a trade; it is not a profession; it is a calling." With approval he quoted Matthew Henry: "Preaching is the best calling but the worst trade in the world"; and Theodore Cuyler: "No royal throne is better or more illustrious."

In notes written by way of preparation for some heart-talks to preachers, he declares:

> "The man who preaches Christ handles fabulous treasures of 'unsearchable riches.' He is put in trust of the most costly jewels. There are no earthly gems in comparison. In the Tower of London I was shown the Crown Jewels of England. I handle greater values every time I preach the Gospel."
>
> "The greatest danger of any church is the decline of the pulpit. Altar fires never burn low until the pulpit declines."
>
> "Then (after stressing the necessity of the preacher's being soundly 'born again') in sanctification by the baptism of Christ with the Holy Ghost, I notice that those who die so dead as to not need another funeral continue 'steadfast in the apostle's faith and doctrine.' 'Much assurance,' something like a gravestone marking the place of crucifixion to the world and the world to you, will be a valuable asset. Be sure that it is 'no more I.' "

"When you undertake to preach without the Holy Ghost, you fail. An unutterable groan in the Holy Ghost is worth more than a sermon without Him."

Though Seth Rees never took manuscript or notes to the pulpit, most of his sermons were carefully and rather fully written out in the study. He left hundreds of manuscripts—the fruit of his best thought, his wide experience and his intimate communion with God. To young ministers he would say:

"Give yourself to reading and prayer. A good general knowledge of the Bible is of first importance. Then fill yourself with Bible history, Church history and the biographies of holy men and women. Don't buy a library; if you do, you will never read it. Buy a book at a time, and read it well before you get another."

He strongly disapproved the use of notes in the pulpit. His advice was, "For your own sake do not permit yourself to lean on paper crutches. It is an injustice to your memory and your powers of thought."

Both in precept and practice he favored sermons of moderate length. With a twinkle he would say, "Blessed is he that maketh short speeches, for he shall be asked to speak again." "Do not preach too long," was his caution. "Long sermons are seldom appreciated by the people." By this, however, he did not mean a twenty-minute "sermonette." He was inclined to believe that "sermonettes" were delivered by "preacherettes." And he was no "preacherette," nor did he want his brethren to be. The average length of his sermons was forty-five minutes.

Seth Rees was at once a man of prayer and a man of action. He was a "practical mystic"; and a "practical mystic," as a thoughtful preacher once remarked to the author, "is the most formidable combination that God ever turned loose in the world." Busy as was his life, it was not without its jealously guarded interludes of solitude and devotion—seasons apart, marked by the "contemplation of the serene and majestic things of God." Among his papers was found, after his death, the following reverie:

> "The solitude of this small study is more to my poor soul than all my social intercourse with humanity. It is here that I am transported to the sunlit peaks where eternal verities blaze and glow in unfading splendor, until all that is terrestrial passes into eclipse.
>
> "Amid misunderstandings, peril, toil and pain, an hour with HIM behind these four walls reveals the great white way and lends the strength to climb heaven's steepest ascents. What strange strength I derive in this solitary nook!
>
> "It is within these sacred walls that I gather strength for a gigantic struggle. It is here that I retire for reparation after the battle."

Yet Seth Rees was no ascetic. What was sometimes mistaken for aloofness and coldness was in reality a natural reserve and modesty. He was fond of the trees and the flowers; he cultivated them in his own garden with tender care, even talked to them, as Francis of Assisi used to talk to the birds. Children, moreover, greatly interested him and drew on his affections. Because of kindnesses he showed to them, declares Rev. R. W. Ives, during a stay in their home in the West

Indies, the Ives children enthusiastically made "Brother Rees" their hero. And much could be written of his love of home and family. From Portland, Oregon, in 1912, he wrote to Mrs. Rees:

> MY PRECIOUS WIFE:
>
> It is lonely this afternoon and I believe I will start a letter to thee.
>
> Great power is on the meetings and people are finding God. Oh, how that pleases me! I often feel that I cannot stay away from home for less than souls. The glory of God and the salvation of souls is the only joy I have in this pilgrim life. There is *no* compensation in money for being away from my loved ones. . . . The sweetness of the Master's service, the joy of having something to cast at His feet in the last great day, bears me up and spurs me on to endure and suffer for Him.
>
> Thou, my precious wife, will reap a far greater share of this glory than I. Thine with the "stuff" and the little ones is the harder place, and thine will be the richer reward. . . . My whole life is bound up in thee. Some day we will march together on a sea of glass and fire. Some day God Himself shall wipe away all tears from our eyes and there shall be no more death, no more sorrow, no more crying, no more pain. All hail that blessed day! May it soon come.
>
> As I think of it now, twenty-four years of my public ministry have been filled with partings—good-byes and heart-aches. But some day parting will be no more and we will never say "Good-bye." Darling, we have walked arm in arm twelve beautiful years; with even sweeter fellowship we shall rove over the hills of heaven and the fields of glory forever and forever."

Easily discernible in this letter is the pathos that tinges the "romance of preaching."

During the last quarter of a century of his life Seth Rees never sang. There was music in his soul, for it rang in the Welsh cadences of his preaching voice, but as for carrying a tune, either by himself or in unison with others, not a note did he sound. It seemed to be a case of a talent put away in a napkin and lost through disuse; in younger years he frequently sang. His appreciation of music was simple and non-technical. He delighted to hear the old hymns simply and feelingly rendered.

He was not without a sense of humor, but his allegiance to Puritan-Quaker principles held it well in check. The author has seen him rock an audience with laughter, not once but twice or thrice in a single sermon, but it was rarely by the stimulus of the anecdote or joke; rather was it a spontaneous humor that expressed itself in sudden sallies of wit, odd comparisons and ludicrous exaggerations. He profoundly believed that the function of the pulpit was not to amuse but to convict and inspire.

Seth Cook Rees was an embodiment of reverence. If his fiery ministry and leadership sometimes seemed to encourage license and "creaturely activity," it was not so intended; and certainly the example he personally set was that of holy dignity. Dead formality is one thing; godly decorum is another. It was the latter that found consistent expression in the conduct of this humble Quaker. While he was presiding over a District Assembly on one occasion, the dinner bell rang and a crowd of people bolted for the exits. He called for order. "Wait a moment," he called. "Don't rush out like a drove of hogs to dinner! Let us be dismissed with a word of prayer." He was grieved by the thoughtlessness, clownishness and fleshliness that are only too evident in many sanctuaries where the people profess to "worship the Lord in the beauty of holiness."

He was strong for punctuality. His children were trained to be at the table on time. His parishioners learned that when a service was announced to begin at 7:30, they would find that service under way if they came trailing in at 7:37. Equally punctual was he in meeting his business obligations. He deeply deplored—and sometimes vigorously denounced—any carelessness on the part of church people, particularly ministers, in conducting their business affairs. He was scrupulous about keeping promises and paying debts.

He cultivated a prayer-life that was Spirit-prompted and Spirit-guided. On one occasion he was seized with a strong burden of prayer for his dear friend, Rev. Charles Stalker, Quaker evangelist, who was then in India. He laid his burden before the "Father Who seeth in secret," never resting until his soul had somehow caught the assurance that it was heard. Not until some time afterward did he learn that his prayer synchronized perfectly with a gravely critical hour in an illness which his distant friend was undergoing. Recovery quickly followed. Charles Stalker has expressed the conviction that on a second occasion of great danger to his life Seth Rees's prayers prevailed in his behalf. This time the intercession was offered with full knowledge of the facts in the case. Word had come that the doctors had given up hope. After the fashion of Hezekiah of old, Seth Rees spread the message before the Lord. Only through "fasting and prayer" was the victory won. Charles Stalker lives to this day, strong in the faith and force of a peculiarly God-owned ministry.

Characteristic of Seth Rees's preaching was a certain bullet-like directness and terseness of utterance. This chapter is concluded with some samples:

"Holiness is the greatest thing in the world. It is indestructible. You cannot burn it, drown it or down it. Persecution does it no damage and difficulties greatly aid it."

"It is a crime to be weak, when power—'power from on high'—is within your easy grasp."

"Opposition wakes up the strongest qualities of the soul."

"Satan tells you to live it and not profess it. He knows that without ventilation it is sure to die. The Bible tells you to do both."

"If you lend your ears to tattlers, they will come home badly soiled."

"If you carry a hatchet, don't forget to take your oil."

"Hell is being peopled for the lack of a radical, aggressive, uncompromising gospel."

"It was not syllogisms nor arguments that convinced the great convocation on Mount Carmel. It was fire!"

"He who sends us against brazen walls will be there to batter them down."

"If you fail to conquer, you are sure to succumb."

"If you can smile through your tears, they will crystallize and adorn your crown forever."

"You must evangelize or fossilize."

"A holiness which is not missionary is bogus."

"The fact that the American pulpit no longer preaches about hell has not cooled it off any."

"If the devil should empty hell to overthrow us, God would, if need be, empty heaven to sustain us."

"I shall never contemplate failure until I am sure that Heaven is bankrupt."

"If God gives you success, do not filch the glory."

"If you seek joy, you will obtain a bubble. If you seek the Holy Ghost, you will secure eternal consolation."

CHAPTER XIV

IN MEMORIAM

"Servant of God, well done!
Thy glorious warfare's past;
The battle's fought, the race is won,
And thou art crowned at last."
—CHARLES WESLEY.

REV. W. C. STONE

Editor of
The Pilgrim Holiness Advocate
Indianapolis, Ind.

A MIGHTY preacher of the old-time gospel of full salvation has been called to his reward; a veteran of a thousand battles and hero of a thousand victories in the Holy War of Holiness vs. Sin has laid down his armor, finished his course with joy, and entered into rest. While thousands mourn his departure here, thousands have welcomed him to mansions above and owned him as the human instrumentality of their eternal salvation.

He was a man of strong convictions as to what is vital in Christian doctrine and experience, and he was uncompromising in his support of these convictions.

He was an indefatigable worker. While he believed God with a mighty faith and relied wholly upon divine power to unctionize his ministry, he worked as though results depended on his own efforts and faithfulness. During many of the days of his illness he kept a stenographer busy transcribing his dictated sermons and articles from morning to night.

Brother Rees was preëminently a man of prayer. He had a missionary vision and carried a burden for the whole wide world. It was his delight to "pray around the world" daily, bearing up to the throne of Grace the faithful missionaries and preachers of all lands, many of whom had been converted and sent out through his instrumentality.

He was unique as a preacher and particularly successful as an evangelist. His sermons, whether spoken or written, were usually brief and always combined a rare degree of simplicity and depth, which made them appreciated by all classes. He preached with the unction and power of the Spirit, frequently reaching climaxes of great and compelling eloquence. Thousands found God in his meetings, many of them redeemed from the lowest depths of sin and becoming marvelous messengers of God to others likewise lost.

As a church we have lost a great leader, and the holiness movement a great preacher of the old-time gospel. His motto was always, "Back to the Bible! Back to Pentecost!" His great cry was, "Fire! Spiritual fire! More fire! Holy fire!"

Dr. H. C. Morrison

Editor of
The Pentecostal Herald
Louisville, Ky.

Seth Rees was one of the most powerful preachers I ever saw on a camp meeting platform. That's where

I frequently saw him in battle against sin for the salvation of souls. He was a tall, broad-shouldered man, with massive head; the appearance of strength was written all over him. His face made you think of the great value of human souls, of the fact of death and judgment, of the seriousness of it all. When he preached there was an earnestness, a directness and power that made sinners tremble and Christians search their hearts.

He held great revivals; people crowded to hear him, went away to tell their friends of his wonderful messages, and invite them to come and hear a most unusual and remarkable preacher. Those invited went, and then called their friends to come and listen to a serious and mighty man who called sinners to repentance and Christians to entire consecration and sanctifying power. People who heard him will never forget him. He sowed the gospel seed in a wide field which will reproduce itself until our Lord shall come.

Dr. John Paul

Co-editor of
The Christian Witness
Chicago, Ill.

Seth C. Rees is gone. He never belonged to the Senate or the Court of St. James; yet he was a world figure. His radiant, fiery ministry was felt in many nations. His transparent testimony exalted Christ, wherever he went. At the time of his passing he was the patriarch of a vigorous denomination of Spirit-filled Christians, the Pilgrim Holiness Church.

His career was a tender romance tinged with pathos. He began life as a Quaker. This was his background; and, to the end, he bore the sturdy marks of the best products of that historic movement, and never forgot to hold himself amenable to the leadings of the Holy Spirit. His first wife was famous as "Hulda the Pentecostal Prophetess." Left bereaved in the prime of life, God gave him the queenly companion who survives him. One of his sons met death in the waters of the deep, if we recall correctly. His elder son, Byron J. Rees, who early became one of America's greatest preachers, passed suddenly from earth in the glory of young manhood. All these and other solemn events gave us in Seth C. Rees a ministry made fragrant and rich by the crucible of sorrow tempered with unutterable consolation and spiritual joy.

By every measurement he was a great preacher, and there were vast thousands to whom he had an anointed ministry.

Dr. H. Orton Wiley

Editor of

The Herald of Holiness

Kansas City, Mo.

Rev. Seth C. Rees was one of the outstanding evangelists of the holiness movement over a period of many years. No greater evangelist ever graced a platform; nor was any evangelist ever more successful in winning souls to Jesus Christ. In his best moments, a peculiar unction rested upon him, and his messages so moved the people, that oftentimes great congregations were swayed by the power of his Spirit-anointed oratory. A rugged warrior, an anointed minister, a fiery evangelist, a successful soul winner, a gifted man of God, an earnest Christian, he has finished the course of his life here, and gone to be with his Lord in that better country, there to receive the reward of his abundant labors.

EDWIN L. KILBOURNE

Los Angeles, Calif.

In

The Oriental Missionary Standard

Much has been and is being written of this wonderful man who walked with God. Much more could be written, but our pen fails us when we recall the hallowedness of the privilege of having had fellowship with one who so radiated the dynamic power and love of God. We loved him; we love his memory. The influence of his life will ever live in our life, and in the work to which we are called.

It was the privilege of the Oriental Missionary Society to number him as one of our Council of Reference, and many have been the letters and conversations in which he has poured out his fervent heart-passion and his love for the lost of heathendom. . . . Brother Rees could touch nothing but what it immediately "caught fire" with the passion and vision that captured and characterized his life and ministry. I believe it was because of this that, in the plan of God, he was identified with so many of the greater spiritual movements of his time.

There are certain men who stand out as representative of the holiness movement in its great calling of revivals and Pentecost. In Brother Rees we have lost an archetype of what God expects of us as a people, and my prayer is that the dangerous compromise-provoking ease of our day may not too quickly efface from our minds and aspirations the memory of this warrior of God.

Rev. Joseph H. Smith

Evangelist
Redlands, Calif.
In
The Pilgrim Holiness Advocate

Fidelity, Fervor and Friendliness were flowers that never ceased to bloom in the character of our brother, Seth C. Rees. Our ministries have touched at high points over a period of forty years: In his Friends Church pastorate, his monumental camp meeting work in New England, in the great Feast of Tabernacles at Mountain Lake Park, in his Pilgrim Church enterprises at Pasadena, and in several varying evangelistic services of the past three or four years. And I am pleased to bear testimony that the manifold variety of his associations and identifications in the modes of his unceasing ministry never impaired nor interrupted these invariable qualities of his character and personality.

Convictions and principles as to Peace, the Faith of the Fathers, the Truth of Holiness and the Honoring of the Holy Ghost were inviolable and impregnable in his faithful soul.

Ecclesiasticism was always secondary to Evangelism with Brother Rees. Churchism and officialism were subservient and ever elastic for the actual saving of souls. His principles were aflame with the passion for the lost, and for the bringing of God's people into the "fulness of the blessing"; and a singular unction attached ever to the fervor of his prayers and usually in the freedom and flavor of his preaching. We have known this strange pathos and fervor in an opening prayer to distil itself through the whole congregation and continue as a fragrance and holy flame throughout the service.

When full three score and ten years of age we have seen him hold on with a glowing and tender tenacity and exhortation until the altar would be filled with seekers. Then he would seem relieved and released, and would slip away for needed rest, leaving sons and daughters in the gospel to do the rest.

Rev. M. G. Standley

In
God's Revivalist
Cincinnati, Ohio

When we heard of the death of Rev. Seth C. Rees, our minds went back and we thought of the great souls who have fought in the thickest of the fight, and who have stood out blazingly for the cause of Holiness. I could hardly wait to read the reports of some of these great men, as they came out in different papers! And as we talked of their passing, we thought: How few remain!

Seth C. Rees was among this number; for he was a prince in the pulpit and God gave him many souls. Also his books and articles were a blessing to thousands and, no doubt, thousands will welcome his Home-coming over there.

Rev. H. J. Olsen

Pastor, Pilgrim Holiness Church

Binghamton, N. Y.

The first holiness sermon I read in a paper was from the pen of Rev. Seth C. Rees. A few months later I was sanctified wholly under the ministry of this peerless preacher of full salvation. In his death I feel a keen sense of loss. I am made to wonder what my life would have been without his message and counsel. When I remember that for more than sixty years he marched on in this holy war without one faltering step, it gives me courage to press on. Today I stand with bowed head, in company with thousands throughout the land, and say in the language of Israel's king, "O my father, my father, the chariot of Israel and the horsemen thereof."

Rev. Charles L. Slater

Missionary-Evangelist
Pasadena, Calif.

More than thirty years ago I met Rev. Seth C. Rees for the first time, at Cincinnati, Ohio. He was among the very first holiness preachers that I ever heard. To me, at that time, he was the greatest preacher in the world, and for preaching the gospel under the anointing of the Holy Spirit, I have yet to hear a greater. His ministry was with power, and in demonstration of the Spirit; great multitudes were swayed; I have seen hundreds rush to a place of prayer after one of his sermons.

I have yet to meet a man who carried a greater burden for souls than did Brother Rees. He not only wept in the pulpit, but in the General Board meetings and in the Executive Council meetings; and when I have been alone with him, I have seen him weep and pray over the lost until my own heart has been greatly stirred to pray for souls.

John R. ("Captain") Lawson

Pastor
Newtown, Cumberland
England

What a mighty preacher of the glorious gospel was the Rev. Seth C. Rees. I have often said he was the mightiest preacher I have ever heard. In his last letter to me he said he hoped to see me again when he visited

England in about two years. Now he has passed on and joined the host of warriors who in their day were mighty in pushing the battle for God and holiness. Earth is certainly the poorer by his passing, but he has left a rich legacy in saved and sanctified souls, living witnesses to the Saviour Whom he loved and served so faithfully.

Part II

ANALYTICAL

CHAPTER I

THE PREACHER

REV. JOHN PENNINGTON

"TO LIVE in hearts we leave behind, is not to die." By this token, Seth C. Rees lives in the affections of multitudes who were blessed by his virile life and victorious ministry. His was no ordinary life. Being his senior by near eight years, I remember him as the chubby, energetic boy. Our parents were friends, and lie buried in the Westfield Cemetery. (This cemetery was a part of the Rees homestead.)

I know something of Seth Rees's perils and problems as he merged into manhood. His conversion to Christ was a remarkable one, as told elsewhere. He began at once to witness for Christ. He conferred not with flesh and blood, but entered his life-long and aggressive ministry. He did not wait for openings for service, but launched out under the Lord's leadership, holding successful meetings in schoolhouses and churches. "A man's gift makes room for him." We were recorded ministers by the same Monthly Meeting, and have been intimately associated in gospel work for these many years. We have been in several meetings and conventions together. He has assisted me in pastorates as evangelist. For some years I was associated with him in the conduct of Portsmouth Camp Meeting Association.

He has meant much to me and my family. He has wisely counseled me in times of peril, and comforted me in times of deep sorrow. His letters have been prized, and his fervent prayers have been a solace. While words cannot adequately express my appreciation of this long unbroken fellowship, I am comforted now in my eighty-seventh year to recall the life of a true man. Some things in this life I suggest as worthy the consideration of the rising generation.

THE GENTLEMAN.

He was a gentleman to the manor born. In his home, on the street, traveling, preaching, socially, everywhere, he was courteous. As a guest, his observance of the proprieties was characteristic of the man. Preachers sometimes mistake boorishness for bravery, and license for liberty. They take, as guests, the whole house, wander from room to room, throw coat on one chair, collar and tie on another, papers on the floor, shoes under the table. Not so, Seth Rees. The writer has a pleasant memory of days spent by Seth Rees and wife and baby Paul in our home. Lack of gentlemanly conduct vitiates life and militates against the minister's influence. May our young ministers emulate the courteous man.

THE STUDENT.

Early in his ministry Seth Rees began a careful study of his Bible. A look at his copiously marked Bible, in use when beginning to preach, reveals his painstaking diligence. In addition to his Bible study, he gave close attention to language, literature, history and biography. Some writer suggests to public speakers the following, "Avoid the abstract, be concrete, tell it in pictures." By his keen observation of natural scenery, methods of transportation, striking historical events, deeds of valor, etc., Seth Rees gathered illustrations that served to make his sermons and writings illuminating. He "told it in pictures." Under the inspiration of the Spirit, his sermons stirred not only the emotions, but produced decision of the will; they "grappled the mind, producing conviction, grappled the conscience, producing contrition, grappled the will, producing resolution." "He that winneth souls is wise."

DISCREET.

One very marked characteristic of this my life-long friend was his discreet conduct in the home, as a guest, as a preacher, as an evangelist, as a citizen. His conduct was remarkably free from any semblance of impropriety. No smirch was ever charged against this godly man.

UNCOMPROMISING.

This man had convictions born of certainty. His thinking and acting were not of the drab sort. A compromise may postpone a crisis, but never averts one. To be neither a coward nor a compromiser is a consummation to be cherished.

A BUSINESS MAN.

Seth Rees was a successful business man. He was scrupulously careful in financial dealings. He knew how to make wise investments. While economical, he was generous with his means. He was opposed to going in debt. In an ordination sermon preached in 1931 he gave this sound advice, "First of all, refuse debt. If you make no debts, you will have no debts to pay." His example and precept are worthy of imitation.

THE TESTED MAN.

As I well know, this man was not free from trials, testings and sorrows. Out of his stony griefs he raised Bethels. He did not parade his sorrows. He carried his sorrows to Christ, and gave his sunshine to the world. He knew how to

> "Yield like the floweret that bends to the gale,
> And bows without breaking when tempests assail."

A FISHERMAN.

The one all-absorbing passion of this beloved co-laborer was his quest for souls. All other plans and pursuits were subordinated to this one objective. While cherishing high ideals of life and conduct, he was no Pharisee. He had a consuming desire to "rescue the perishing." None were so low, so degraded as to repel or discourage him. His great heart of love yearned over the unfortunate. He prayed much and fervently before entering the pulpit. His sermons were burning messages, tenderly and tearfully uttered. He expected victory and was not defeated or disappointed. His altar calls were those of faith, confidence and expectancy. Doubt in the pulpit begets doubt in the congregation. He did not say, "If any one has a need, come," or "Is there one?" His calls were, "Let everyone having a need, come." Following these fervent appeals, thousands responded. God grant that we may have a generation of preachers who can catch men. "They that be wise shall shine as the firmament and they that turn many to righteousness as the stars forever and ever."

CHAPTER II

THE LEADER

Rev. Paul W. Thomas

Camp meetings and Seth C. Rees were apparently made for each other. Although I did not clearly discern this at the time, something of it came to me when, prophet-like, he first walked into my line of vision on a camp meeting platform. Still in my teens and a convert of barely eight months' standing, I was in that happy stage of experience where all the preachers were great and wonderful men. His name meant little more to me than did the names of the others, but my first glimpse of him warned me that he was going to be different. He was. The picture of that first Sunday morning is still very fresh and vivid. It would have been difficult for me to have told you at the time just why, but in my own mind and heart I assigned him the place of a prophet—an Old Testament prophet in New Testament times.

The passing of time through more than a score of years has wrought many changes. Eventually I came to know more of Seth Rees and his ministry. Sometimes I hardly knew what to make of him, but as I was thrown into more intimate contact with him in the work of the Lord, I discovered that back yonder I was not far from the truth; for Seth Rees was indeed a prophet—a real

New Testament prophet. No other description quite fits him.

Some men have certain natural qualities of leadership and, regardless of where you place them, these qualities are soon apparent. This was true of him, so really and obviously, indeed, that no great depth of human understanding was necessary to make the discovery. How far this spirit of leadership might have carried him in the world, had he not found Christ, we may only imagine. Something of it was already evident long before he was converted. I recall hearing him, in private conversation, deplore the fact that as a young man he had been a leader in wickedness. The hint is all I ever got, for the very thought of it humbled him and he never would enlarge upon it. That wayward career was fortunately nipped in the bud by his early conversion and his steps were turned towards God and Heaven. What he might have been, however, in business, politics, or in other spheres of human activity, seems scarcely worth speculation in view of the leader that God made of him.

He was indeed a leader. People felt it when they saw him. They knew it when they heard him. He seemed to have been born for leadership and was doubtless called of God to fill the high office that he always held. But he was preëminently a devotional leader and his finest triumphs were always in the realm of the moral and the spiritual.

In keeping with his frequent counsel to the young and aspiring about him, he never waited for things to turn up; he turned them up. He did things. Nevertheless, there was little of the active organizer or the bustling official administrator about him. It was always perfectly clear to him that business should be attended to and he wanted it cared for promptly, but he preferred to wash his hands of the mechanics of the task so that he might devote his energies to the main issue. One could never reproach him over this, for he gloried in his attitude and it was hard on him when the Gospel train was delayed and when business was slow in taking the siding.

He was often a puzzle both to friend and foe. Perhaps there would have been nothing hard to understand about him had they accepted the simple and most vital explanation of his life and ministry. Humanity sometimes likes to hunt for a man's motives, and folk were always searching for his. Failing to find what they looked for, they reasoned that he had cleverly concealed it from them. But the fact is, there were no such motives as they sought. He was simply the Lord's prophet, first, last, and all the time. Pass over the fact that his leadership was so truly devotional and spiritual, and you miss the key to his life. Much that you will find is bound to appear without reasonable explanation. View him in any other light than this and he will often appear as an eccentric; a very able one, to be sure, but an eccentric just the same. Explore his career with this to guide you and the varied events of that long ministry fall into orderly and inspiring sequence.

In this, his leadership among men of his rank is quite unique. Many of his ability and marked success would have chosen to develop around them organized forces into which their personalities would have been largely projected. His personality was felt, of course, and was penetrating enough, but the only organization he cared for was just that which an ardent lover of the truth would build.

It was only natural for his brethren to call him to important official posts. These calls he did not always accept, but when he did, it was only as he believed it clearly his duty to do so and because it appeared to present new opportunities for the Gospel. In his own heart and mind such relations were only secondary and he saw to it that he maintained those relations in such a way that he could quickly and completely sever them whenever he discovered that he did not have a free channel for the full salvation message which he preached. Perhaps in no other one thing was he more misunderstood than in just this, particularly because he rarely bothered to explain the matter to the public.

His great query to his own heart was always, "Is it right?" Sometimes he pondered matters long and carefully. But once the issue was clear he proceeded according to the light God gave him. And proceed he did, regardless of objections and objectors.

His people were of pioneer stock. His father and his uncle cut the first road into what is now Westfield. He, himself, possessed the soul of a frontiersman. Just as the biting blades of the settlers' axes felled the hickory and the oak of Indiana, so his Gospel axe has cut through many a knotty tangle. Thus he, too, was a blazer of trails and a builder of roads. Somehow he always managed to live on a spiritual frontier. He liked nothing better than to stir things up when there was a lull. It always seemed to me that he rather liked the feel of the weapons and tools of the Gospel in his hand.

Lovers of ease and wrongdoers winced under such leadership. Any attempt to assume a neutral position proved impossible when he was around, if there was a moral or a spiritual principle involved. Men were forced into some kind of action. One simply had to take one way or another. I frequently wondered if this was not the reason people so quickly fought with him or against him. In moral conflicts he neither asked for quarter nor did he offer any. There were no neutral shades in his color scheme. Well do I remember being with him in official meetings when, to satisfy his own mind, he forced every man present into an open committal on the issue involved. Such a soul is bound to be a force among men. Such rugged crusading as this is a very potent kind of explosive.

While he refused to fellowship in any degree what he knew to be wrong, yet I never knew him to show any bitterness over it. He just produced an air of finality that made you know he was through, but was ready to pray for everybody.

Perhaps nothing brings out the significance of his spiritual leadership quite like the results produced among those to whom he ministered. There have been other evangelists in America who have preached to larger congregations and who can number their converts, often in a single campaign, by the thousands. But it is doubtful if there is an evangelist in America among whose converts there is a larger percentage of established saints and workers for God. People arose from his altars to do things. They went from hearing his messages to bring things to pass. Rescue homes, Bible schools, slum missions, camp meetings, holiness churches, and foreign missionary efforts seemed at times to spring out of his very footprints. For verification of this one need only turn to the story of his life. Hundreds of living witnesses, at the time this is being written, need no other proof than that of their own memory.

In connection with this aspect of his leadership particular reference should be made to his part in the foreign missionary work of our present day Holiness Movement. As astonishing as it may appear at first glance, nevertheless, when the complete history of the foreign missionary work carried on by our Holiness people is written, it is more than probable that the figure of Seth C. Rees will appear to be among the greatest of missionary leaders in more than fifty years, perhaps in a century. But more of this appears elsewhere.

He was a Christian to the core. This is the tribute of many and I write these words sincerely and deliberately. They are the truth. Doubtless this was the foundation of his greatness, for if he was a great leader on the platform and in the presiding officer's chair he was a greater at home and in his private life. I have gone with him for a meal when he brought heaven and earth together while returning thanks at the table. He had the knack of being able to turn our morning worship at the Church offices into a camp meeting inside of five or ten minutes almost any time.

The shoddy and the cheap in religion sickened him. Long-winded folk with little to say wearied him. Carnal strut and display never had his approval. Little-souled folk who made much ado about nothing bored him. But he delighted in true spirituality and reveled in genuine freedom with the lowliest kind of folk. He prized the solid, tested things. Sometimes in private he would ask for one of the old hymns and get shouting happy during the singing. I have known him to get blessed dictating a sermon for publication.

Seth Rees was what he was because God made him so. The secret of the Lord was with him. It often appeared as though he possessed unlimited resources both of mind and spirit. And he did. They were the resources of Heaven. God honored him with a rare and fruitful leadership because he honored God.

"They that be wise shall shine as the brightness of the firmament; and they that turn many to righteousness as the stars forever and ever." Distant stars project their light across the unmeasured miles and years. As truly as God has declared it, so the Christian leadership of Seth C. Rees is shining still across the years and the miles.

CHAPTER III

THE MISSIONARY

Rev. G. Arnold Hodgin

Among redeemed man's noblest deeds stands first the hurrying with tireless feet to get the gospel to the unevangelized millions of earth. God has spoken of such labors as "beautiful." But it is imperative that the missionary shall not only get to men: he must go with a personal passion for souls, and a message that will reach their hearts and consciences. He must experience in his own life the efficacy of the healing balm which he offers as the only remedy of the sin sores of mankind anywhere in the world.

Those who know the facts about the varied and indefatigable labors of Brother Rees, in the pastoral field, will remember that he was never satisfied with the usual round of church work. He was not content just to labor for the perpetuation and growth of even the most spiritual church. He was of the firm and abiding conviction that for a local church, as well as a denomination, to approximate its rightful function, it must be unequivocally committed to a strong and thorough missionary program. He did not waver in his belief that any church that expected to come up to the standard of holiness should at least do two things. It should make large contributions to the cause of missions; and it must, in fulfiling its part of the great commission, send forth from its own fold, fire baptized and Spirit filled gospel heralds to the regions beyond. He was gratified to see from the church which he founded, and of which he was pastor for a number of years, equipped and efficient workers sent to different foreign fields. It was well known that this same church, under his leadership, gave such sums for foreign missions that he could and did state that far more was given for the furtherance of the gospel than was required to carry on the work of the local congregation. Yet during those years the pastor's support and the church expenses were never neglected. There was usually money in the treasury. While he co-operated in magnanimity with all worthy enterprises, still he was of the strong persuasion that if the holiness movement could be kept from selfish propaganda and the octopus of mechanization, there would be no lack of funds or laborers for the mission fields. He could find no place in his soul for wild and extravagant presumptions in the name of faith, but which lacked that great and necessary element; still he held to the conviction that careful and unselfish enterprises, if properly propagated, would generate a genuine faith that would bring the backing of the tithes and offerings of God's people.

Perhaps no man in the realm of full salvation movements has been, through the medium of missionary correspondence, a greater blessing and comfort to lonely, tired, over worked and under paid missionaries, than was Seth Cook Rees. His pen was not only facile and fertile; it was remarkably dynamic with a Spirit energized love and sympathy for those who were in the toils of hard and arduous labors on the far-flung battle lines. His letters to many missionaries, scattered all over the world, were outstanding epistles of encouragement and brotherly love. They were classics. Terse they often were, to the point of abrupt brevity, but they were packed full of soul food and sympathy. Blessing and uplift for drooping spirits sparkled from his pen point, like brightest morning sunbeams among the dewdrops on daffodils or a daisy flecked meadow. Laconism found an elegance in his letters, as in his impromptu speeches on right occasions, that few men have equalled. Oftentimes in our travels in recent years in many lands, men and women who we knew had been going through some deep waters of struggle and test have told us with buoyant spirits that, in the most needed hour, a letter had come from "Brother Rees" that had wonderfully helped them on the way, and strengthened the soul for renewed efforts in sacrificial service and in warfare against the powers of darkness. They will marvel at the aptitude of the message borne to their need in a dark hour, and bless God for such a man as "Brother Rees." Such art in letter writing is rare in these days. But now that his arm has dropped nerveless by his side, and the pen can no longer be used, many will remember those heartening missives. They will sorrow because he no longer writes them. Heaven only will show the beauty and blessing of his missionary correspondence.

A strong personality strongly influences others. A great personality indwelt by the Holy Spirit never fails to move others toward a place of exalted service. Many outstanding accomplishments have been thus begun. Some men who have gone to mission fields and there have done exploits for the kingdom, were greatly moved by the life, love and letters of Rev. Seth C. Rees. Many names might be given to show the numbers now on the field, or who have gone to the upper glory, who were influenced by this mighty missionary soul to go on and spread the gospel of complete salvation in places where it had not been heard. Rev. and Mrs. Charles C. Cowman, and Rev. E. A. Kilbourne, who through the Oriental Missionary Society have done such a great work in the Orient, were greatly influenced by "Brother Rees." An excerpt from a recent letter from Mrs. Charles C. Cowman, who since the home going of her illustrious husband, and his co-worker Rev. Kilbourne, carries on the work most nobly, is given here.

"What shall I say about our beloved 'Brother Rees'? He was such a friend to all the missionaries, and such an inspiration! Thirty-three years ago, before we left our homeland for Japan, Brother Rees laid his hands upon us, setting us apart for the work whereunto our Lord had called us. Throughout those years he was ever our close friend. His gracious ministry in the Orient will ever live on throughout the years. His messages were blessed to our native brethren, who caught some of his fire. His great heart was filled with love for the lost heathen. We feel that our loss is beyond any words that can be expressed. May God grant to us who remain some of his missionary passion."

Rev. C. O. Moulton, who laid down his life in a noble work in the West Indies, owed to "Brother Rees" a debt of gratitude for so strongly influencing him in his young manhood to go and do "Exploits in the Tropics." Rev. and Mrs. Francisco Soltero, who have seen such phenomenal transformations among the Aztec and other Indians in Mexico in recent years, say in a letter, "We have always considered him (Brother Rees) as the real founder of our work in Mexico, which, we rejoice to know, he loved and prayed for to the last." On another page they write, "His letters were full of courage, and alive with hope and possibility." Many other missionaries were in the same manner helped and inspired.

Prayer is a mighty force. He who pours out his soul in impassioned pleadings for others actually influences the heart of God, Who sometimes leaves the leverage of His mighty arm to the potency of prayer. Seth Cook Rees had many friends on the mission fields. For these, as well as others, he poured out his very being in supplication, so tender and yet so strong, so pleading and yet so insistent, so passionate and yet so intelligent, that hearers were often moved to awe. Those prayers reached the throne room of heaven, and unexpected help was rendered in remote lands. His heart-throbs of tender love, mingled with much weeping, touched the heart of God, and the power of Divine love pulsated through the lagging footsteps of the missionaries. Then they rose up to fight new battles, and to render service with a new heroism.

Like Cornelius, moreover, his "prayers and his alms" went up together "for a memorial before God." Few persons knew how liberal he was as a steward of the modest measure of this world's goods which was his. In *The Pilgrim Holiness Advocate,* August 17, 1933, Mrs. Francisco Soltero, reporting on the work in Mexico, wrote:

> "One young Aztec Indian preacher, whose support for one year has been provided for by our sainted General Superintendent, has been having unusual success. Surely the prayers which were behind that support are being answered. In the month of May, the very month when our Superintendent was called to his heavenly reward, this young Aztec saw sixty-five seekers and in the month of June had seventy. Already 135 souls, and only two months gone! Will other saints not take up the great work of intercession where our General Superintendent laid it down? How we need men and women to help us in mighty prevailing prayer."

Missionaries must go, and get to men. Seth Cook Rees went, not only all over his native land, preaching the unsearchable riches of Christ, but he went to the ripened harvest fields abroad. He was none the less a missionary because he did not spend all his days in remote fields. He went for a season, and great was the harvest. He, with members of his family, made an extended missionary journey to the different European and Oriental fields. There he rendered an abundantly fruitful service in preaching. There he led many hundreds to Christ. Later, with Mrs. Rees, he made a trip to the West Indies and contiguous lands, where he witnessed marvelous deliverances through his fiery ministry. During those last days upon earth, when his physical sufferings were equalled by the surging sufferings of a soul that, held back by physical weakness, so longed to fly to the ends of the earth, he had one all consuming desire which he often expressed. It was that he might make another missionary tour through Mexico and Central America, and there expend his waning strength for souls in need. But God willed a much better thing for him—a glorious journey to the homeland in the skies. Missionary indeed he was, to the very end of a transformed and God-appointed life.

Part III

INSPIRATIONAL

CHAPTER I

THE HIGHER ENLIGHTENMENT

A SERMON

BY SETH C. REES

"The eyes of your understanding being enlightened; that ye may know what is the hope of his calling, and what the riches of the glory of his inheritance in the saints." EPHESIANS 1:18.

THIS is a portion of one of the few prayers that the Apostle Paul made with his closet door ajar. We know that he prayed day and night, sometimes, like his Lord, "with strong crying and with tears;" but we know the wording of only a few of his prayers. We do know that he was filled with unutterable longing that his converts and brethren might come to know and understand the glorious "hope" of their "calling" and the magnitude of their inheritance through Christ.

He well knew that if their eyes were fully opened to their splendid heritage, it would dry many of the tears of earth, fill their hearts with the joy of the Lord and their mouths with shouts of victory. He was sure that a vision of their possessions and their prospects in Christ would release their grip on the perishable things of this world and would cause them to rise up and embrace eternal verities.

I

Notice the first clause of the text: "That the eyes of your understanding being enlightened."

This—just this—the Holy Ghost does when He comes to our hearts. He enables us to see clearly. Much that was mysterious, obscure or uncertain is now as plain as high noon; it becomes an absolute verity. In this age of rapid transit, sharp competition, keen, quick action, nobody wants to stand and listen to a man who is uncertain about the matter of which he is talking. Three million dollars worth of business was transacted between Pasadena, California, and New York City in half an hour over the telephone. Thinking men want quick action. If you want to interest them in religion, you will have to *know* about it yourself.

It is refreshing to hear a man who knows what he is talking about. On the train I often hear one person trying to tell another about California. The party talking may have been in the state for a week or a month and may have seen something of two or three towns or cities. It is wonderful how well he can talk—how much he can say that isn't so! After I have lived in California nineteen years it is not easy for me to listen to a man who knows little more about it than I do about the South Pole. If you want to interest and help people spiritually, yours must be a convincing testimony. You must know!

One of the mightiest incentives to Christian work is a knowledge of the Holy Ghost, an illumination and an assurance concerning those things that Christ has made available to us and to others. There can be no genuine enthusiasm without convictions born of certainties. A knowledge of the magnitude and the unfading eternity of your inheritance in Jesus will cause you to lose interest in the uncertainties of time. A young man of means fell in love with a poor girl who was all "togged out" with cheap jewelry. He indicated to her that he was a bit ashamed of it. She said, "Well, John, I like it, and it is the best I can afford, and I can fool a few people with it." The next time John came he gave her a fine plush box, and when she pressed the spring she found it full of real diamonds. It did not take her long to dispense with the "Pittsburgh glass."

The son of Alexander the Great was in the midst of dissipation when he heard of his father's death. He at once arose to his feet and declared, "I shall have done with all of this, for it ill becomes one who is heir to a throne." No one can catch a glimpse of his high relation to God as a Christian, his spiritual sonship with all its exalted favors, the vast wealth of his estate in Christ, without breaking with the paltry things of earth and becoming enamored with unfading and unfailing riches.

An old miser accumulated a large fortune. He was afflicted with blindness. Consulting an oculist, he was told that he had cataracts, but that they could be removed. In reply to his inquiry about the cost he was told that the charges would be so much for each eye. He agreed to have one eye operated upon, and the operation was successful. When asked if he would have the other eye treated, he said, "No, it is too expensive. I will get on with one eye." This is the language of many Christians. "It costs too much!" Thousands of professors of Christ would rather see in part, would rather see "men as trees walking," than to pay the price of complete abandonment to God through which they might come into the fulness of the enlightening Holy Ghost.

II

Now let us notice the second clause of the text: "the hope of his calling."

What is this calling? And what is the hope of it? In Philippians 3:13, 14 Paul says, "Forgetting those things which are behind, and reaching forth unto those things which are before, I press toward the mark for the prize of the high calling of God in Christ Jesus." Our calling is "the high calling of God."

1. It is indeed an "high calling" which calls us to *sonship* in the family of the everlasting Father. John stands amazed in the presence of it. "Behold, what manner of love the Father hath bestowed upon us, that we should be called the sons of God. . . . Beloved, now are we the sons of God, and it doth not yet appear what we shall be." (I JOHN 3:1, 2.)

It was a "high calling" when Israel was called from the bondage of Egypt. She was not only called *from* but called *to*: *from* the galling yoke of slavery and the brick fields of servitude *to* the sunny heights, fruitful vineyards and luxuriant harvest field of Canaan. But what was that compared with our calling? We are called *from* the "far country" of disobedience, guilt and shame *to* the fellowship and feasting of the Heavenly Father's house and to divine heirship—"heirs of God, and joint heirs with Christ," His only Son. Ours is to be an "inheritance incorruptible, undefiled, and that fadeth not away."

Angels have a high calling. They are called to serve, to fly at Jehovah's bidding and obey His behests; but all that is not to be compared with the privilege of spiritual sonship which is offered to sinning men. Angels about the throne have never known the depths of sin. Not so with us. Our calling is high because it reaches us in such depths and lifts us to such heights. We wear the purple of royalty who once ran in tatters and rags. We sit at the King's table who once grovelled among the swine and the husks. "Beloved, now are we the sons of God!" Servants lodge in the servants' quarters; guests are restricted to certain rooms; but sons have access to every room in the palace.

2. Ours is a "high calling" not only because we are called to sonship, but because we are called to *holiness*. "For God hath not called us unto uncleanness, but unto holiness." (I THESS. 4:7, 8.) "According as he hath chosen us . . . that we should be holy and without blame before him in love." (EPHESIANS 1:4.)

Clearly, the purpose of God is that we shall be "holy and without blame before him in love." In fact the whole movement of divine energy in redemption is to bring men back to holiness. Holiness calls for the elimination from the heart of man of all that antagonizes God; the conformity of the whole man to the will of God.

There is a heresy abroad that would make holiness easy—and cheap. It teaches believers that since the new nature is holy, one need not bother about the old nature. It matters naught what sins are committed, they have nothing to do with the new nature. Others attempt to make holiness easy by claiming and teaching that the sinful nature is simply covered by the imputed righteousness of Christ. That is like cleaning (?) the barnyard by covering it with a blanket of snow. But Christ came to "destroy the works of the devil." The "works of the devil" are chiefly in the human heart. These are to be "destroyed." Jesus taught us to pray, "Thy will be done, on earth as it is in heaven." Inwrought Christian holiness is God's answer to that prayer. He calls us to be holy; He stands ready to make us holy.

3. We are not only called to sonship and to holiness, but to *heaven*. This is our "hope." "Wherefore, holy brethren, partakers of the heavenly calling!" (HEBREWS 3:1.)

Ours is a pilgrimage through a "vale of tears." The poet has called man a "pendulum between a smile and a tear." But in heaven they weep no more. Critics say they do not know much about heaven. I do. John told me more about it than can be put in a thousand volumes when he said, "There shall be no night there." I know what night is in reality and I know what it is the emblem of—darkness, mystery, gloom, ignorance, error, sin. For many years I have been a poor sleeper, and all my nights are too long. How glad I will be to stand on the "river of life" in a country where there is no night. Darkness will never cast its shadows over the fair hills of that cloudless clime. Sickness and grief are worse at night. How we long for the dawning of the day! How transcendently glorious and welcome will be the first rays falling across the eastern hills on the dawn of the New Day! This is our hope!

We are called to all the wealth of heaven—our "Father's house." We are transformed into His image here; we are going to be translated into His glory there. Eventually our calling is going to bring us into the imperishable splendors of that City where disappointment, sorrow, sickness and death will never come.

III

Now I want to notice the third clause of our text: "the riches of the glory of his inheritance in the saints."

Christ makes His inheritance ours. He shares it with us; He plants it in us. Let us itemize some of His bequests.

1. The inheritance of *victory*. Jesus won a complete victory over the devil in the wilderness, in the garden, on the cross and at the wide open grave. He overcame "the world, the flesh and the devil"; and His victory is a part of our inheritance. By His indwelling through the Spirit, His triumph becomes ours. He fights our battles. In His strength we march on our knees from victory to victory and from glory to glory. "Because greater is he that is in you, than he that is in the world." (I JOHN 4:4.) Jesus overcame, and would make over-

comers of us. "To him that overcometh will I grant to sit with me in my throne, even as I also overcame, and am set down with my father in his throne." (REV. 3:21.)

2. Another feature of our inheritance is *peace.* When Jesus was about to leave the world, He left a very wonderful legacy to His people. It was such as no earthly prince or potentate could have devised. None of the great, renowned or wealthy ever left such a testament. It was not kingdoms, crowns or scepters. It was not silver, gold or estates; not titles, dignities, stocks or bonds. It was peace! "My peace I give unto you!" This is more than peace *with* God; the disciples had that. Such peace always goes with reconciliation and regeneration. This was more; it was nothing less than the peace *of* God, even "the peace of God which passeth all understanding." "I will keep him in perfect peace!" Great indeed is the heritage of peace.

3. Still another bequest is *joy.* "These things have I spoken unto you, that my joy might remain in you, and that your joy might be full." (JOHN 15:11.) His joy in the soul is a divine fountain, superior to all earthly environments, overflowing upon all the desert world around us.

What more trying position could one be placed in than that of Paul and Silas in the jail at Philippi? Backs torn; lying on a cold, filthy stone floor; feet fast in the stocks! But look at them. Listen to them. At midnight they have evening prayers, and they are so blessed that they break into praises. They sing. Their joy is so deep and so up-surging that nothing can cap it. It overflows. Its song is so loud that God hears it. It is a sort of serenade under His window and He gives them an encore. One stamp of His foot, and they are released from their stocks, their prison doors are shaken from their hinges, and the prisoners are free. That is joy with strength in it.

Beloved, let this joy, a gracious bequest from Christ, be your strength. It is a part of the "riches of the glory" of that "inheritance" which He wants to share with the saints.

CHAPTER II

BENEFICENTLY BRUISED

A COMMENCEMENT SERMON

By Seth C. Rees

"Bread corn is bruised."—Isaiah 28:28.

Nothing appears so perplexing and paradoxical to this old world as real Christianity. Its philosophy differs so widely from all human philosophies and human reasoning that men either stand amazed or turn to ridicule. Christianity takes man down to the depths of self-abasement and then lifts him to the very heights of victorious power and most glorious achievements.

In no literature, classic or heathen, can you find such seeming contradictions as appear in the Christian Scriptures. "Sorrowful, yet always rejoicing;" "Poor, yet making many rich;" "Having nothing and yet possessing all things."

It has pleased God to begin His greatest undertakings with nothing. Not only in creation, but in salvation He begins with nothing. He takes pleasure in contradicting human wisdom, human possibilities; in transacting His greatest business without capital.

In the words of the text which I have chosen we are introduced to one of the greatest enterprises of heaven; one of the most mysterious and paradoxical processes of grace.

BENEFICENTLY BRUISED

I

The subject is the process of breadmaking. The inspired writer has taken a parable from nature. The grain, which we know as wheat, was called corn in those days. When he says, "Bread corn is bruised," we at once think of broad wheat fields. The waving, golden grain has ripened in the summer sun. We think of a crew of harvest hands who harvest the grain and bind it into bundles. Then we think of the threshers who come and, by a severe process, separate the wheat from the straw and chaff. Next we have the milling day—the severer process of being crushed between the upper and nether millstones—when the wheat is converted into fine flour. In our thinking we then fly to the domestic kitchen, to the kneading and the rolling, the pounding and waiting overnight for another pounding, and then the roasting-oven.

We see that breadmaking is quite a science, most of which is a severe process. In oriental countries the instruments used differed widely from those used today, but the process was the same. "Bread corn is bruised."

In oriental countries they used, and in Arabia to this day they use, at least four kinds of threshing instruments. The different instruments are for threshing the different grains. Fitches and cummin were not threshed like wheat and corn; they were not worth it. The method of threshing was mild or severe in proportion to the value of the grain. Wheat and corn were put through a severe process, for they are breadstuff.

II

This parable has a striking application to Jesus, Who declared Himself to be the "Bread of Life." Also His disciples, who are commanded to feed perishing humanity. Jesus was bruised from the cradle to the grave. A Baby, with the most refined nature on earth, must lie among the cattle and move among the rougher class of men. While yet an infant He was forced to flee to Egypt for His life. Think of the distance from the highest heaven to an oxstall, then down to Egypt among strangers. The tendrils of His sensitive nature were whipped and bruised all through life. "He was bruised for our iniquities." How much that means!

Like the golden grain, our Lord was cut down and ground under the heel of the enemy. By the fiery ordeal of the Garden, the Judgment Hall, and the Cross He was transformed into the Living Bread, which giveth life to the souls of men.

The greatest national prosperity, moreover, has come out of the greatest adversity. Nations of inhospitable climate have had the ascendency over those of tropical and luxuriant lands. A rugged climate stimulates the inhabitants to greater exertion and develops the ruggeder qualities of strength and energy. This pushes them forward to conquest and to victory. The highest national qualities have always been developed by opposition and oppression. It was these that pressed our fathers of the Revolution to heroism and independence. Israel lost nothing by Pharaoh's oppression. The more they were oppressed the more they multiplied and grew.

What is true of Christ in this regard and of the history of nations, is true of His disciples. We are members of a Divine Body, of which He is the Head. We are left here to fill up the measure of His suffering. We, like our Lord, must undergo a spiritual development. This can come only by a severe discipline.

III

This is a day for which you have toiled and to which you have looked forward for a dozen years or more. It should be a day to which you will look back forever as one marking a notable epoch in your lives. You should receive something of vastly greater value than the compliments of this faculty or the applause of this congregation. These flowers will fade tomorrow. If you have the right conception of life and adjust yourselves to the enginery of heaven, you may be transported to heights of broader visions, loftier ideas, and nobler service than you have ever known. But—"bread corn is bruised."

I have known talented and cultured Christians of beautiful character, endowed with naturally charming personalities and graces, who were like the golden grain waving in the summer sun. Many of the graces of nature had to be cut down, threshed and milled in order that the fruit of the Spirit might grow. The harvesting, winnowing, and milling process is not joyous; but it is essential to the breadmaking.

Poverty, hardship and misfortune have pressed many a life to moral heroism and spiritual greatness. Difficulty challenges energy and perseverance. It calls into activity the strongest qualities of the soul. It was the weights on father's old clock that kept it going. Many a headwind has been utilized to make port. God has appointed opposition as an incentive to faith and holy activity.

IV

The most illustrious characters of the Bible were bruised and threshed and ground and roasted into bread for the hungry. Abraham's diploma styles him as "the father of the faithful." That was because he stood at the head of his class in affliction and obedience.

Jacob suffered severe threshings and grindings. It was between two millstones that the meanness was taken out of him. Joseph was bruised and beaten and had to go through Potiphar's kitchen and Egypt's prison to get to his throne.

David, hunted like a partridge on the mountain, bruised, weary and foot-sore, was ground into bread for a kingdom. Paul never could have been bread for Cæsar's household if he had not endured the bruising, whippings and stonings. He was ground into fine flour for the royal family. The irons on his arms were the brands of quality, like *"Pillsbury's Best."*

Paul not only stood the tests in Christian activity, but in the solitude of captivity. You may stand the strain of the most intense labor, coupled with severe suffering, and yet break down utterly when laid aside from all religious activity; when forced into close confinement in some prison house.

That noble bird, soaring the highest above the clouds and enduring the longest flights, sinks into despair when in a cage where it is forced to beat its helpless wings against its prison bars. You have seen the great eagle languish in its narrow cell with bowed head and drooping wings. What a picture of the sorrow of inactivity.

Paul in prison. That was another side of life. Do you want to see how he takes it? I see him looking out over the top of his prison wall and over the heads of his enemies. I see him write a document and sign his name—not the prisoner of Festus, nor of Cæsar; not the victim of the Sanhedrin, but—"the prisoner of the Lord." He saw only the hand of God in it all. To him the prison becomes a palace. Its corridors ring with shouts of triumphant praise and joy.

Restrained from the missionary work he loved so well, he now built a new pulpit—a new witness stand—and from that place of bondage come some of the sweetest and most helpful ministries of Christian liberty. What precious messages of light come from those dark shadows of captivity!

V

Think of the long train of imprisoned saints who have followed in Paul's wake. For twelve long years Bunyan's lips were silenced in Bedford jail. It was there that he did the greatest and best work of his life. There he wrote the book that has been read next to the Bible. He says, "I was had *home* to prison and I sat me down and wrote, and wrote, for joy did make me write." The wonderful dream of that long night has lighted the pathway of millions of weary pilgrims. That sweet-spirited French lady, Madam Guyon, lay long between prison walls. Like some caged birds that sing the sweeter for their confinement, the music of her soul has gone out far beyond the dungeon walls and scattered the desolation of many drooping hearts.

Oh, the heavenly consolation that has poured forth from places of solitude!

Six thousand Quakers were in prison at one time. Their goods were confiscated and their homes broken up. The jails were to them like gilded mansions, as through the prison bars rang their happy songs. Not only were the turn-keys converted, but people passing on the streets. At the end of one year George Fox was recapitulating, and said: "We have had a good year. There has been no time in the year that there were less than one thousand of our people in jail." "Bread corn is bruised."

What was it that the poet said?

"Stone walls can not a prison make,
Nor iron bars a cage;
His presence e'en a cell can make
A holy heritage."

VI

In Arabia they do not thresh fitches and tares; they are not worth it. If you see some one living in ease, without trial, do not envy him; if he were worth harvesting he would be threshed. If you are beaten and bruised and banged and pounded, just remember that God is making fine flour for the breadline. Those with smaller trials make only second grade flour. Many furnish no bread at all.

When David was made king of Israel at Hebron, the Philistines came up against him. Before he was promoted they did not consider him worth attacking. When you hear the Philistines after you, remember that perhaps they have heard that you are about to be promoted. If God orders you to lead some forlorn hope, or to defend some lone citadel, it is because He has trusted you with a great honor. God's eyes are never taken from you in trial. The way you take bruises determines the brand you are to bear. If you would be *"Pillsbury's Best"* you must suffer without complaint.

It is the bruised oyster that creates the pearl. You may be rock-ribbed, with girders of imported blue steel. You may go through the furnace with credit, or you may be a cake unturned. What is more obnoxious than bread half baked? I have seen the cook test her cake with a clean broom-straw. If nothing sticks to the straw it is well done. God has ways of testing those who are roasting.

VII

My context says, "He will not ever be threshing it." There will come a time when all tests will be over.

I have read of forty ancient martyrs who were offered a chance of life on a frozen lake in the north of Italy. They stood naked and shivering in the bitter cold. One by one they sank to death for Jesus' sake. Finally one grew weary and decided to recant. He went ashore and told the sentinel who stood guard in the lodge. The sentinel looked at him in amazement, and said: "Fool, if you had seen what I have seen tonight, you never would have thrown away your crown. I go to win it," and the guard passed out to take the recanter's place. He had seen a company of angels hovering over the scene with forty crowns for forty victors.

"He will not ever be threshing it." Some day, some bright, beautiful day, the storm-clouds will crack wide open. Even now the blacker the storm-cloud the brighter the rainbow. His bow of promise spans the universe. It will stand after the arches of heaven have fallen. He is coming back to earth again. He will not fail to claim His own. "The foundation of God standeth sure, having this seal, the Lord knoweth them that are his."

He will catch His waiting Bride away. God Himself will wipe away all tears from our faces. That is one of the things He will not trust an archangel to do. In that day, that beautiful day, this class may march together on the sea of glass mingled with fire in that grand review where those who have fought well at the front, and suffered without complaint, will awaken the applause of the highest heavens.

"BREAD CORN IS BRUISED!"